JUDGE LYNCH

PATTERSON SMITH REPRINT SERIES IN
CRIMINOLOGY, LAW ENFORCEMENT, AND SOCIAL PROBLEMS

A listing of publications in the SERIES *will be found at rear of volume*

PUBLICATION NO. 55: PATTERSON SMITH REPRINT SERIES IN
CRIMINOLOGY, LAW ENFORCEMENT, AND SOCIAL PROBLEMS

JUDGE LYNCH

HIS FIRST HUNDRED YEARS

BY FRANK SHAY

HV
6457
S5
1969b

With an Introductory Essay
LYNCHING AND RACIAL EXPLOITATION
By Arthur F. Raper

133941

Montclair, New Jersey
PATTERSON SMITH
1969

SBN 87585-055-3

Library of Congress Catalog Card Number: 69-14945

LYNCHING AND RACIAL EXPLOITATION

LYNCHING AND RACIAL EXPLOITATION

By Arthur F. Raper

IN the recent widely heralded mob outbreak in San Jose, California, some observers, chiefly in the South, are finding welcome proof that lynching is not a sectional problem. The explanation of the South's eagerness to share the ignominy of lynching with other sections will be clear to anyone who will sit beneath a spot map of lynchings in the United States and study the record.

Although many lynchings have occurred out-

Publisher's note. This paper, published here for the first time, was written in 1934 by the author of *Tragedy of Lynching* (University of North Carolina Press, 1933, reprinted as Publication No. 25, Patterson Smith Reprint Series in Criminology, Law Enforcement, and Social Problems [Montclair, N.J., 1969]). In *Tragedy of Lynching,* Dr. Raper investigated and reported in dispassionate sociological detail the circumstances surrounding lynchings. The present paper contains Dr. Raper's reflections on the broader political and social implications of his findings. These observations, of interest in their own right, illustrate the prophetic value of solidly based social research.

side the South and many mob victims have been native-born whites, lynching is increasingly a Southern phenomenon and a racial one. In the last decade of the last century, approximately 18 percent of this nation's lynchings were outside the South and 32.2 percent of the victims were white. During the decade just passed, less than five percent of the lynchings have occurred outside the South and scarcely ten percent of the victims have been white, including Mexicans and other non-natives who account for upwards of half of the mobs' white victims. In the typical lynching the victim is a Negro, the lynchers are native-born white, and the courts punish no one.

The double lynching at San Jose was the least typical of last year's mob outbreaks. For that reason it was spot news for the nation and for the world: the victims were white men, and they were lynched in California; thousands of newspaper columns would have been devoted to this story even if Governor Rolph had been as speechless as the Sphinx. Two other lynchings of the year productive of headlines were those at St. Joseph, Missouri, and Princess Anne, Maryland, both within the upper fringes of the South. The victims were typical enough, but a serious effort was made to punish the lynchers—which seldom occurs in the major lynch belt — and so these cases, too, made news for more than a day. The only two lynchings inside the South to make the national headlines were the first two of the four at Tuscaloosa, Alabama, when the Judge called out the militia to protect from mob violence three white International Labor Defense lawyers who appeared to defend the accused Negroes. The other twenty-two lynchings of the year occurred within the lynch belt and within the orthodox lynch patterns, and were almost totally lacking in widespread news value for the white press.

With the Negro, America's "tenth man," furnishing 90 percent of the mob victims, one logically looks to the Southern racial situation for the underlying causes of lynching. Formerly an instrument of popular justice in frontier communities, lynching is now primarily a technique of enforcing racial exploitation — economic, political, and cultural.

Economic exploitation of the Negro by the American white man is as old and as continuous as the Negro's presence on American soil. Slavery, peonage, lower wages, restricted work opportunities, and differential public welfare facilities are expressive of his principal economic handicaps in the developing American scene. Widespread organizations like the Ku Klux Klan and local ones like Atlanta's Black Shirts, have openly advocated a kind of "white supremacy" which tends to limit Negro employment to such work as the whites do not choose to do. Certain new types of work, such as driving buses and streetcars and operating textile machines, have been restricted almost solely to whites. Moreover, under the general economic stress of the last few years the Negro has been losing ground at an accelerated rate in his erstwhile occupational monopolies.

The Negro's economic exploitation has been greatest and crudest in the Black Belt of the lower South, where still remain more than mere vestiges of slavery — man's most complete system of exploitation. The usual methods of plantation commissary bookkeeping leave the tenants unable to know the amounts of their debts, thus making it possible for the agents of unscrupulous planters, of whom there are more than a few, to make such entries as they like, to charge whatever price they prefer for items, and to collect whatever interest they desire.

The creditor-planter can virtually name the price that the tenant receives for the farm produce with which he repays his debts. Not infrequently the storable farm crops produced by the tenant are taken over by the planter at fall wholesale cash prices and sold back to him later at spring retail credit prices. For example, the tenant's bushel of corn which settles a 30 cent debt at the end of one year's farming represents a new debt of about twice that amount at the beginning of the next. To enforce this transaction, planters provide no corn cribs or other storage facilities at tenant houses but rather make it mandatory that cotton, corn, peanuts, and so on be deposited in the storerooms at plantation headquarters.

Such practices, justified by those who control the plantation on the basis of the workers' improvidence, make it very difficult for the tenant to rid himself of debt. To perpetuate this and other types of exploitation, the planters in many areas follow the gentleman's agreement of not hiring a new wage hand, sharecropper, or tenant unless the change meets with the approval of his last landlord. Thus robbed of his normal right to move, the propertyless rural man can escape this quasi-peonage only by fleeing the community, which involves considerable risk. Threats of flogging, murder, and lynching follow and sometimes overtake the "debtor" who "slips off like a thief." If he gets safely out of its reach, the violence originally meant for him may descend upon his relatives and friends. No Negro is safe when some member of his group has challenged the plantation controls.

But, it may be said, the plantation and its controls are of the past. True, the Black Belt, in company with every aspect of the nation's socioeconomic structure, has undergone great changes in recent years. With these new conditions have come some new techniques of exploitation. The Federal services have been variously administered, depending to no small degree upon the attitude of the local county committee which administered them. In some communities the cash loans received by the individual farmer from the Government for feed, seed, and fertilizer have indeed been used by the borrower to buy feed, seed, and fertilizer at cash prices. But in more extensive areas the Negro tenant, upon instruction of his landlord, surrendered his check, getting back the cash as the landlord thought he needed it; or getting it back in feed, seed, and fertilizer at spring credit prices. In the former case, the tenant paid double interest, 8 percent to the Government for the money and an additional 8 or 10 percent to the planter for keeping it for him! In the latter case, the planter alone profited, for he utilized the tenant's borrowed money to buy at cash wholesale prices the feed, seed, and fertilizer which he sold to the tenant at spring retail credit prices; thus the planter made a sizable profit off the tenant who provided him with his operating capital.

In many communities, exploitative practices have not been lacking in the local administration of Red Cross flour and cloth. In most rural Black Belt counties the plantation has been the unit of administration, and usually the plantation trucks carried the flour and cloth to the plantation headquarters for distribution. Not uncommonly the recipients willingly repaired fences or did other occasional work for their landlords who "secured" the flour and cloth for them; in short, considerable quantities of free Red Cross flour and cloth were virtually bought from the landlords by the tenants. Current reports on the operation of the Public Works Administration and Civil Works Administration show that, as usual, in numerous Black Belt counties local practices have arisen which keep the Negroes from sharing equitably in the benefits of these services. The significant thing about these newest techniques of economic exploitation is that they are so essentially like the old ones.

Racial exploitation, with its broad economic base, reaches into all the vital political phases of community life. State, county and municipal governments — the legal agents of the white population — have developed their own methods of sharing in this exploitation. For example, the Negro's educational opportunities and hospital facilities are limited. He usually receives poorer police protection, and in many instances a smaller grocery order from the relief headquarters; he seldom sits on a jury, and almost never has a voice in the allocation of public funds. Throughout the counties of the Black Belt the public money spent on the education of the white child is three to sixty times that spent on the Negro child; other public services are administered on similar racial differentials. In services rendered, as in control, it is truly a "white man's government."

These discriminatory and exploitative laws and practices, most pronounced in the cotton states where most lynchings occur, have well known political antecedents: the effective leaders in pre-Civil War days upheld slavery; after Appomattox they resented and, when possible, openly defied the Reconstruction-Carpet Bag regimes; to rid themselves of the fruits of Northern control, they defended the terroristic methods employed to intimidate and disfranchise the Negroes; later, under the shibboleth of "white supremacy" they enacted laws and perfected party procedures to preserve Negro dependency.

Within the general pattern of the Negro's political exploitation, which is South-wide and in some respects well-nigh nationwide, are many conflicting details. These minor differences come from the varied backgrounds of the community units and from the prevailing attitudes of the articulate white leadership. Though the Negro is politically and economically dependent in either case, there is a qualitative difference in the exploitation in a community controlled by the poorer white element as contrasted with a community controlled by the scions of the landed aristocracy.

Most insidious of all has been the cultural exploitation of the Negro; it enforces his political impotence and economic helplessness. For instance, whatever humor there is in most of the white man's popular stories about the Negro tends to be based on some veiled allusion to him as an amiable simpleton, lacking in morals, intelligence, and ambition. The black-faced characters common in vaudeville, grade and high school entertainments, and sometimes even in those of the church, are good drawing cards for white audiences primarily because white people like to see servile and docile Negroes in ridiculous roles. All this rests upon certain rationalizations, chief of which is that the Negro has been ordained to a position of subservience and servitude.

The cultural exploitation of the black folk has been something of a profession. Businessmen and politicians, and sometimes church leaders, have capitalized upon race prejudice to gain larger profits through lower labor costs or to make their political and institutional leadership secure. The South's Watsons, Bleases, Heflins, and Vardemans in politics, and many leaders in industry and other fields, have not been irrational, from their restricted view. They saw a harvest for themselves in the exploitation of the race situation. The success of the professional Negrophobes has rested to no small degree upon conditions which they have been instrumental in creating and maintaining. These Frankenstein-ish prophets have been looked upon as statesmen and even as saviours by the typical white South-

erner, personally acquainted only with Negro
farm laborers and domestics, most of whom are
illiterate or nearly so, are crowded into small
quarters, live on a scanty ration, and seldom
have adequate facilities for bathing or enough
clothing. According to the popular assumption,
they are also morally unclean. This, too, it will
be said, cannot be helped, for they have within
them no basis for morality; they are essentially
shiftless, carefree, irresponsible, child-like. As
runs the common belief, they can scarcely profit
by their experiences of yesterday or anticipate
their needs for the morrow. Therefore, if "regular hands" are wanted, the employer had best
pay a small wage, for they will work only when
hungry. Furthermore, according to this popular
estimate, all Negroes are essentially alike —
they steal, they lie, and the males are inclined
to commit certain serious crimes, the worst of
which is assaulting white women.* Despite their

*The widespread obsession of white men that Negro
men need to be restrained from raping white women
seems to arise from the not uncommon practice of
white men consorting with Negro women. This practice
was most prevalent prior to Emancipation, judging by
the mulatto children born to slave women. Mulatto
children born to white women have been few in number.
It would seem, therefore, that when white men insist
that the lynch threat is needed to protect white woman-

personal knowledge of numerous Negroes not of this stereotype, most Southern white people proceed on the assumption that all other Negroes are of this type, and thus implicitly create a situation in which no Negro can be certain he is outside the reach of inescapable and aggravated dependency.

In sore need of some religious sanction for his deliberate exploitation of the Negro, the typical Southern white man turns to the Bible — particularly to the cursing of Canaan by his drunken grandfather, Noah, as related in the latter part of the ninth chapter of Genesis — for the explanation of the Negro's economic and cultural situation no less than his color. (When told that the passage makes no mention of anyone being turned black, a fatherly Georgia white man insisted that it did. He got his Bible, but could not find the desired passage — the Bible is a big book. When the Genesis passage was read to him, he said: "Well, maybe I don't know exactly what it says, but I know what it means." He hesitated, then added: "If anyone don't be-

---

hood, they are assuming a sexual imbalance created by their own behavior, and so fear that the neglected parties, the Negro men and the white women, will tend to get together.

lieve in the Bible, I don't want to talk to him.")

Having arrived, through wishful thinking, at the assumption that the Negro is something less than a normal human being, the majority of white people logically and openly treat him so. "To be sure," said the white principal of a rural Mississippi high school, "he should have justice as a human being, but in accordance with the kind of human being he is."

In brief, the role of the Negro is rigorously defined. He has poorer schools and a disproportionate share of illiteracy, fewer public health nurses and greater morbidity, smaller parks and higher juvenile delinquency rates, dimmer streets and greater crime frequency, small houses and more illegitimacy, limited employment and longer breadlines, longer hours and smaller wages and higher death rates. And the white people who thus defined "his place," though themselves paying too dear a price for it, insist that the Negro stay in it. They react violently, and often hysterically, if they think he is either getting out of it or showing effective dissatisfaction with his economic dependence, political impotence, and cultural subservience. Lynchings and other destruction of the Negro's life, labor, and property are in essence but the more violent expressions of the white man's determination to continue the economic, political, and cultural exploitation of this minority racial group.

Though the annual crop of mob deaths in the United States tumbled down from 255 in 1892 to 8 in 1932 (rising to 28 in 1933), the noose still dangles before the eyes of the American Negro. He is in forty times as much danger of being lynched as the white man. He still has "his place" in most communities.

And it is by no means an accident that the same decades of Southern history which record the greatest decrease in the number of lynchings also record numerous statutes and ordinances and community practices directly and indirectly prescribing the Negro's working and living conditions. The defiantly extra-legal controls of the mob have been partially displaced, particularly in urban communities, by these more "respectable" controls, which have grown up to meet the demands of an ever-increasing number of Southern white people who while still assuming that the Negro must be kept in "his place" have become ashamed of the crudity of direct mob control.

By prescribing the Negro's activities, such

statutes, ordinances, and other non-violent controls have lessened the white man's need of resorting to overt violence. Along with these limitations of the Negro's opportunities to compete, and partially because of them, has come considerable displacement of colored workmen by white workmen. This shift, dating back into the last century, has been greatly accelerated by the depression, until at present, all across the South, the whites are steadily moving into fields of employment formerly looked upon as "Negro work." All sorts of methods have been resorted to. In Atlanta, for example, the courts were induced by an organized white effort to oust the Negro bellboys from hotels so that whites might have their jobs. Some months ago, an attempt was made in New Orleans to displace Negro longshoremen by limiting this occupation to qualified voters; and logically enough, the whites demanding this councilmanic action would keep the Negroes from the polls.

The substitution of quasi-legal controls for mob controls, however, is by no means the sole explanation of the decrease in the number of lynchings, for these same decades have been characterized by marked educational and cultural advancement. And lynchings are now least common in the larger towns and cities where the greatest cultural gains have occurred. Mob deaths are most common in communities economically and educationally below the average, where the countryside is sparsely settled, where the status of the races is least defined, where the quasi-legal methods of control are least often used, and where peace officers and court officials are most answerable to local sentiment and demands. As a matter of statistical record, the Negro in one of the South's half-dozen largest cities is in scarcely one-fiftieth as much danger of being lynched as is the Negro who dwells in one of the South's 250 most sparsely settled and backward counties.

The Negro city-dweller, in fact, is scarcely in as much danger of being lynched for the murder of a white man, by far the most frequently reported single cause of mob violence, as is the rural Negro dweller for such trivial accusations as stealing bootleg liquor, slapping a white boy, talking back to a plantation overseer, resisting arrest when unarmed, getting into an altercation with white men over a mulatto woman, arguing that the truck he owned was better than the one driven by a white man. Such were the accusations against six of the Negroes lynched during the past year, while four more were faced with no accusation at all: George Green, killed at his farm home near Taylors, South Carolina, by a band of masked men who went there at midnight upon the request of his land-lord who had become irritated at this Negro tenant for insisting upon a settlement; Richard Marshall, riddled with bullets and hanged near Newton, Georgia, to show Negroes that this is a white man's country; Fell Jenkins, unaccused, flogged to death near Homer, Louisiana; and James Royal, shot to death at Decatur, Alabama, near the scene where another Negro, rushed out of the county for safekeeping, was alleged to have committed a crime earlier in the day.

Quite contrary to the popular opinion that most lynchings are caused by assaults on white women, the murder of white men — many of them self-defense killings like the one last June at Warrenton, Georgia — has been the cause of about one-third of all lynchings since 1890, whereas scarcely one-sixth of the mob victims have been accused of rape. All accusations of rape and attempted rape combined account for less than one-fourth of the mob deaths as re-ported in the white press. Thorough investiga-tions of numerous recent accusations of rape

xxi

and attempted rape, moreover, demonstrate clearly that many of these were false. It is an appalling fact that in many localities, particularly in rural areas, almost any Negro man's life is at the mercy of almost any white woman's word; witness the recent lynching (August, 1933) of the paralytic, Dennis Cross, at Tuscaloosa, Alabama.

While it is significant that many Southern metropolitan areas are tending to raise themselves out of the kingdom of lynch law, it must be remembered that much of this advance has been bought with a price. So long as the poorer urban whites find in non-violent controls effective means of ridding themselves of the Negro's competition, there is little provocation for violence. But what are the limits of these peaceable methods of resolving the racial conflicts which continuously arise? In New Orleans, the peaceable attempt to drive Negro longshoremen from their jobs has failed; the Negroes are still working along the wharves. Will the whites continue their efforts? Will an ordinance displacing the Negroes be enacted? If the whites are unable to get what they want through the non-violent methods, will they resort to violence? The race riots in Tulsa, Chicago, Wilmington, Philadelphia, and Atlanta grimly remind us that cities are not immune to violence.

Just now, too, the further use of the white South's typical "legal procedures" for handling its racial problems may be greatly complicated. Even the present efforts of the Federal Government in the direction of a single standard of wages and of relief are looked upon as dangerous precedents by many white Southerners. But the typical Southern employer now finds himself with mixed emotions. He is a Democrat, and the administration which launched the National Recovery Administration and stands back of the relief standards is Democratic. Moreover, Democracy's Chief refers in a neighborly way to Warm Springs, Georgia, as his second home.

Opposed to the Southern white man's sentimental and traditional bases for his patriotism are the race differentials to which he is accustomed in every field of life. The theoretical single standards of the New Deal are inimical to the white South's rationalizing assumption that the Negro does not need as good a diet, as good a house, or as good a school as the white man. It is altogether doubtful whether, under other political circumstances, the great mass of Southern employers would cooperate at all in any Federal program which proposed the same wages and the same relief for the two races. It is not without meaning that this section's traditional loyalty to the Democratic party now constitutes the chief hope for success in Dixie for the National Recovery Administration, the Civil Works Administration, and the Farm Security Administration with its supervised "rehabilitation loans." We see how precarious are the chances of the New Deal's ironing out of racial differentials in the South when we realize that any widespread local support of these proposals is contingent almost solely upon those same peculiar sectional hopes and fears which have created and sustained the "Solid South." Most significant of all, in so far as the New Deal is successful in abolishing or lessening racial differentials, it will tend to undermine the theory of innate racial differences upon which rest the most prevalent patterns of present-day race relations.

There are, of course, "Lily White" Republican groups scattered across the South.* The very

*For an instance involving one of these groups in which violence resulted, see Raper, *Tragedy of Lynching*, chap. 10. The term "Lily White" originated with the old-line Negro Republicans but came into common use in Southern newspapers.

name bespeaks their impotence to deal constructively with the racial situation.

A comparatively small number of Southern white leaders are now pointing out that this region can never obtain its rightful place in the economy of the nation until the Negro is paid fair wages. They maintain that low wages for the Negro inevitably mean low wages for the white, too; and that low wages, by undermining the buying power, consign the section to economic stagnation as contrasted with the regions with higher wages. Can this enlightened minority group in the South maintain its position against the appeals to race fear and prejudice which the reactionary forces always rely upon when questions arise which involve the status of the races?

The South is heir to still other disturbing factors. Certainly it requires no prophet to see what would become of the whole structure of legal racial segregation should the white jury system of the South be declared unconstitutional. Practically all of the South's racial issues, nominally settled by legislation and party practices, would inevitably be up for reconsideration and readjustment. Though the making and administrating of laws, the issuing of licenses, and the allocating of public funds are matters of a political nature, their economic and cultural implications are evident to the Southern white man. He has insisted on a racial differential. If present procedures are thwarted, what substitute methods will be employed?

It will be recalled that physical violence was resorted to in the last decades of the last century when the Negro was being disfranchised by terrorism: he was then driven out of the statehouse and courthouse by force, and subsequently kept out by statutes, ordinances, and party practices. The question raised here is whether these statutes, ordinances, and practices which were called into being to safeguard and perpetuate the fruits of terrorism will continue to retain the nominal affirmation of the United States Supreme Court. Though the Negroes put up no united aggressive resistance to their disfranchisement, it is a well-known fact that they have not felt altogether kindly towards their political dispossessors. An appreciation of this fact is one of the keys to an understanding of the South's hysterical fear of Communistic efforts among the Negroes.

The South is facing — who knows what? Widespread unrest in Dixie is more than a mere possibility. Even before the depression the plantation system was disintegrating rapidly; now a great proportion of the planters are on the land largely at the sufferance of their creditors; thousands of sharecroppers and farm tenants who received Red Cross rations and cloth in the winters of 1931 and 1932 and Federal relief in 1933 and 1934 and who have been financed in recent crops by credit from the Federal Government are beginning to realize that the plantation owners are not indispensable as once thought. For lack of the required mule and plow, thousands of other propertyless rural dwellers are finding it impossible to qualify for the Federal loans, and consequently are unable even to plant crops. While the landed Southerners and the landless Southerners barely hold onto a crumbling plantation system, the traditional rural South seems to be passing from the scene.

With machines to mow hay, thresh wheat, and shell English peas and half-ripe lima beans, thoughtful Southerners wake up every morning wondering what will become of its millions of human cotton pickers — largely marginal laborers already — once an efficient mechanized cotton picker has been put on the market. Centuries ago unneeded workers could sail across the oceans to new continents; decades ago they could push across the new continent to secure free land; years ago they could satisfy the need for manual labor in the metropolitan areas. But where can they go today? Earlier they were attracted away; now they are being driven away. Earlier it was the more alert and adventurous individuals who left home to try their luck elsewhere; now it is the most dependent and least skilled families (wage hands, sharecroppers, and dependent tenants) who are losing their precarious niche in the cotton economy. What will they do? Will they march on the county courthouse, the statehouse, or the national capitol? There is little prospect they will permanently shuffle down to the swamps and push up on the sides of the gully-washed hills to eke out a bare existence. There is little prospect at present that Federal "rehabilitation loans" for dependent farm families will be more than a stopgap operation. No, inevitably and inexorably the stranded rural dwellers will gravitate to the urban centers, where they arrive virtual refugees, ill-prepared physically, educationally, politically, socially and culturally for life there.

The high likelihood that the South's methods of handling its "race issue" will be challenged in these times of imminent technological development raises many an unknown. Will the South have the ability to maintain decorum while evolving new bases for race relations? What will happen in the haven cities of the South, North and West?

Contents

5

CONTENTS

Preface

"TO HELL WITH THE LAW"

LYNCHING has many legal definitions: It means one thing in Kentucky and North Carolina and another in Virginia or Minnesota. For the purpose of this work it is defined as the execution without process of the law, by a mob, of any individual suspected or convicted of a crime or accused of an offense against the prevailing social customs. The state of Minnesota clearly defines it as the killing of a human being by the act or procurement of a mob. In Kentucky and North Carolina the lynch-victim must have been in the hands of the law or there was no lynching. Virginia defines it simply as murder and ordains that every person composing the mob, upon conviction, shall be punished by death.

There is more than the simple dictionary definition of lynching. Behind every lynching, beyond the destruction of the unfortunate victim, is the debasement of citizenship, the crucifixion of justice and democratic government, the prostitution of public officials,

7

and the depraved behavior of the mob-members. The effects of a lynching on the mind of an observer, especially a child, cannot be estimated. The consequences of sadistic practices put human relations on a considerably lower plane. Dr. A. A. Brill states: "Anyone taking part in or witnessing a lynching cannot remain a civilized person."

It is seldom that a mob gives voice to its creed as did the one outside Covington, Tennessee, in August, 1937: when urged by the sheriff to let the law take its course, it cried, "To hell with the law!" It is not only the cry of the lyncher but of every other type of criminal.

Since 1882, when lynchings were first recorded, through 1937, the toll of the mob has been 5,112 victims. More than four fifths of these were Negroes, of whom less than one sixth were accused of rape. Lynchings have declined from a high of 235 in 1892 to a low of eight for 1937. The decrease was not constant: in 1932 the number fell to ten only to rise to twenty-eight in the following year. It is an inevitable fact that during the coming years certain Americans will meet their deaths at the hands of mobs.

Lynchers are criminals in the same sense that murderers and kidnapers are criminals: lynching is a criminal activity, and to be put down it must be considered as such. Obviously law enactment is not enough; rigid enforcement is necessary and it must be backed up by a public sentiment against the crime. Even the most serious protagonists for a Federal law against lynching do not believe that it will stop the practice. They point out that proposed Federal legislation leaves the apprehension and punishment of lynchers to the state, that it only makes recalcitrant states abandon their do-nothing policy, and that it forces peace officers to resist the mob beforehand and to prosecute it afterwards. It seeks to guarantee the humblest citizen the due process of the law and the equal protection assured him by the national Constitution. It provides that cowardly and unfaithful public officials may be fined and imprisoned, and that the people of the county who permitted the murder be made liable for monetary damages.

Such a law will not eradicate the crime of lynching, but it will convince peace officers that they must not release their prisoners to a mob and that the lynch-minded must suppress their sadistic desires: it will serve as an effective curb on a crime that many Americans condone.

It is almost impossible to verify statistics relating to lynchings. For this work the author has gone to several sources: from 1882 to 1888 the accepted totals are those compiled by Cutler from the files of the Chicago

9

Tribune, and from 1889 to 1937 the records are those of the National Association for the Advancement of Colored People. Some independent research has not materially changed these figures. For prevented lynchings, the estimates of Monroe N. Work, of the Department of Records and Research at Tuskegee, have been accepted. In many communities there are forces strong enough to suppress news of lynch-executions; in others the bodies of the victims are destroyed or secretly buried, and the members of the small mobs sworn to silence.

For my research I have used the published material of many individuals and organizations. That I have been materially aided by the work of James Elbert Cutler, Walter White, Arthur F. Raper, and James Harmon Chadbourn is apparent and herewith acknowledged. Organizations such as the National Association for the Advancement of Colored People, the Southern Commission on the Study of Lynching, the American Civil Liberties Union, the Industrial Workers of the World, the International Labor Defense, and the Workers' Defense League have been helpful in letters and documents loaned. To the Federal Writers' Project thanks are due for a leave of absence to complete this work.

PREFACE

To Alfred Hartog I am indebted for considerable aid and valuable time devoted to research, to Miss Richetta G. Randolph and Julian B. Thomas for the loan of valuable material and helpful suggestions. To my wife, Edith Shay, my thanks for counsel and help in the arrangement of material and for the compilation of the bibliography and index.

F. S.

JUDGE LYNCH

Chapter One

THERE WAS A JUDGE NAMED LYNCH

IT was not until forty years after his death that the name of a Virginia soldier in the War for Independence was given to the practice of summary punishment he had introduced as a war-time measure. It is a long way from the mild, repressive measures of Colonel Charles Lynch, who was known to some as Judge Lynch, to the legendary figure bearing his name whose known victims now number 5,112,[1] many of whom went to their deaths by methods almost inconceivable. Judge Lynch, the real, was an honorable patriot, a Quaker whose religious scruples forbade the taking of human life even in war; Judge Lynch, the legend, whose code contains only the sentence of death, is a savage American whose practices bring shame to all other Americans.

A century of lynching, with more than 5,000 recorded victims in a little more than half that time, has placed America in an unenviable position before the

---

[1] January 1, 1938.

entire world. It has done incalculable harm not only to our reputation as a civilized country but to ourselves, our manner of thinking, and the welfare of future generations.

No nation, ancient or modern, has been entirely free from mobs and "mobocracy." But mob-law is not necessarily lynch-law, whereas lynch-law is always executed by mobs. The mob is always the result of a temporary or permanent breakdown or failure of a social system; it is invariably accompanied by violent death, be it the death of an individual or of a class. That there are justifiable mobs is beside the point; certain diseases are cured by inoculating the patient with a virus that, if administered to one in good health, would in itself produce death.

Aberrations of justice are not distinctively American. Summary justice has been meted to individuals throughout history. There are isolated instances in modern Europe, but these bear the stamp of genuinely spontaneous action on the part of the people who, outraged by his criminality, fell upon the offender and put him to death. The imperfect evidence at hand would indicate that it was invariably the guilty person who was lynched and not, as is so often the case in this country, one who was merely suspected or accused of criminality.

Other commentators and historians have sought to

connect American lynching practices with those that existed in Europe before and shortly after America was settled. They have discovered a likeness in such institutions as the feudal Vehmgerichte of Westphalia, but the Fehmic courts were secret tribunals established for the preservation of the true faith, the promotion of peace, and the suppression of crime. All their operations were veiled in mystery: their secret spies penetrated to the remotest corners of Germany, their judges were unknown, their judgments were swift and their execution certain. The Vehmgerichte bear a closer resemblance to our Ku Klux Klan and other repressive groups than to our general and more democratic practice of lynch-executions.

The Lydford laws, gibbet or Halifax law, Cowper and Jeddart justice, and the Scotch burlaw bear a strong resemblance to our Frontier Justice, to the Vigilantes in their original conduct. All these practices originated in a genuine and popular need and through the lack of regularly constituted law courts. That they were later prostituted to ulterior and selfish purposes is within this thesis. Venice's Council of Ten, Castile and Aragon's Holy Brotherhood were regularly constituted and legal, even if repressive, bodies, and their edicts were accepted laws. Only in Czarist Russia did the practice of lynch-executions somewhat similar to ours prevail. It was the custom to take horse-thieves

17

and club them to death, to tie them to the tails of young horses, which were ridden off at a gallop; or the lynchers would fasten the victim to a log while the women punctured his skin with sharp instruments until death ensued.

What is now known as lynch-law, the court of Judge Lynch, and Judge Lynch himself were unknown to the earliest colonists. Summary justice was meted to misbehavers of almost every type and to those guilty of offenses not covered in the common law. It was an accepted practice, not because there was no formal law, but because formal law was undergoing a severe change. Today the stool-pigeon is the accepted accomplice of all police regulation; in those early days an informer was invariably in the service of the crown and therefore anathema to all patriots who, when he was unmasked, undertook to flog him and to hold him up to popular exposure and contempt. But the man who laid on the lash, who applied the tar and feathers, or who ordained that the victim be carried on a rail was known as Squire Birch.

Many New England communities had officials known as "warners-off," whose duty comprised the investigation of all newcomers as to character, religion, goods, and other local requirements. If in their wisdom they felt the newcomer was not one who would add luster and wealth to the community or if his family were liable to become public charges, the warners-off went into action, giving a five-day warning to clear out. Beyond that their powers of office did not carry them. If the ostracized did not leave within the prescribed time, the people figuratively took the matter into their own hands and brought the head of the family before Squire Birch, who ordained the method of chastisement. After the administration of justice, the offender was taken to the town's limits and ordered never to return, under penalty of "worser" treatment.

Summary punishment was also exercised against Indians who overstepped treaty bounds, against chronic drunkards and wife-beaters, and, in certain communities, against non-churchgoers and, in others, tobacco smokers. Later, when matters became tense between the colonists and their British oppressors, violent treatment was used against loyalists—informers who accepted the crown awards for pointing out patriots or revealing the persons and lairs of smugglers.

The origin of the legendary Judge Lynch has been obscured by the legend-makers. Ploughing through histories and memoirs, the last words of oldest inhabitants and first settlers, folklore, and the works of contemporary writers brings out the fact that there was a Judge Lynch and that an act of the Virginia legislature was known as Lynch's Law.

Charles Lynch, who was to give his name to a jurisprudence he never practised nor would have tolerated, was born in 1736, at Chestnut Hill, his father's estate in Bedford County, upon which a part of the city of Lynchburg now stands. Lynchburg was not named for Charles Lynch but for his elder brother, James. The father, an Irish redemptioner, had been sold to a planter, and the young immigrant, when his redemption period was completed, married Sarah, the daughter of the house, a professed Quaker. After the planter's death, the mother joined the Society of Friends; James, the oldest son, became possessor of the estate; and the two younger sons, John and Charles, took parcels of the family land that lay near the border. Charles followed his mother into the Cedar Creek Quaker meeting, and the records of the congregation show that on December 14, 1754, the young man and Anne Terrill first published their intentions of marriage. Later the young couple established their home on the Staunton River, in what is now Campbell County.[2]

For some years Charles was an active member of the

2 "The Real Judge Lynch," by Thomas Walker Page, *Atlantic Monthly*, December, 1901.

Society of Friends and, for a time, clerk of the monthly
meetings. Later the exigencies of the times, 1767,
caused him to accept public office, and he became un-
satisfactory to the peace-loving Quakers, who dis-
owned him for taking solemn oaths, contrary to the
order and discipline of the Friends. It was in that year
that Charles Lynch was elected to the House of Bur-
gesses, where he held his seat until the colony became
independent. In 1776 he was a member of the convention that sent the instructions to the delegates from
Virginia to the Continental Congress, which exercised
a decisive influence on the movement for independence.

At the beginning of the War for Independence his
Quaker principles still influenced his actions to the extent of keeping him out of active military service. Mr.
Page says: "He did not enlist in the army, partly because of his Quaker principles, but chiefly because his
presence was imperatively necessary at home. He had
to rouse the spirit of his constituents to support the action he had advocated in the convention. He had to
raise and equip troops for the army. He had, as it were,
to mobilize the forces of his country, and attend to all
the duties of a commissary department. In addition,
he had to make some provision in the event of an attack
from hostile Indians."

In 1778 he had sufficiently stifled his Quaker scruples to accept a commission as Colonel of Militia and to organize a regiment.

It was as officer commanding this home-guard organization that his name was given to a species of summary justice. The theater of war had shifted to the South, and both armies were in desperate need of horses. The prices paid were so high that gangs of rustlers made horse stealing a lucrative practice. The local courts were only examining courts and the single court for final trial of felonies sat at Williamsburg, more than two hundred miles away.[8] To take the prisoners thither, and the witnesses necessary to convict them, was next to impossible. Frequently the officers in charge of prisoners would be attacked by outlaws and forced to release their men, or be captured by British troops and themselves made prisoners.

As practically all of the horses were stolen from American farmers to be sold to the British forces, the thieves were, for the greater part, Tories. Colonel Lynch placed the matter before his friends and neighbors, and it was decided to take things into their own hands, to punish lawlessness of all kinds, and, so far as possible, to restore order and security to their community. It was not the "Vehmgericht" in any sense, but a war-time measure. Colonel Lynch was appointed

[8] Cutler: *Lynch-Law.*

22

presiding justice, and three neighbors, Captain Robert Adams, Jr., Colonel James Callaway, and William Preston, associate justices. Colonel Lynch's home was to be their courthouse.

It was the custom of this court to have the accused brought face to face with his accuser, permit him to hear testimony against himself, and allow him to summon witnesses in his own defense. If acquitted, he was allowed to go, with apologies, his inalienable right to sue for false arrest intact. If he was convicted, he was sentenced to receive the Law of Moses, which is forty lashes less one, on the bared back; if he did not then shout "Liberty forever!" he was strung up by the thumbs until he did so. The most convinced Tory shouted for liberty without further ado.

The chorus of a once popular patriotic song current in Virginia after the war runs as follows:

"Hurrah for Colonel Lynch,
Captain Bob and Callaway!
They never turned a Tory loose,
Until he cried out 'Liberty.' "

Later the Tories were greatly encouraged by the news of the British invasion of Virginia, and they proposed to seize and hold for Lord Cornwallis the stores collected by Lynch for General Greene's army in North Carolina. Colonel Lynch, with his regiment, was on the point of setting out to oppose a British army under Benedict Arnold when news of the conspiracy was brought to him. Manifestly it would not do to whip the conspirators, make them shout "Liberty forever!" and turn them loose, nor could he order them put in irons and taken along with the regiment. The Colonel sought the advice of his fellow-justices, and it was decided to sentence them to terms of imprisonment of from one to five years, and the leader, Robert Cowan, was additionally fined £20,000, due to war-time inflation less than $1,000.

That was the real Judge Lynch.

After the war, the Tories who had suffered at the hands of Colonel Lynch and his associates, threatened to prosecute them. To avoid lawsuits and to settle a war-time affair for the future, Colonel Lynch laid the whole matter before the Virginia legislature. After a long debate, for there were many unreconstructed Tories yet in the legislature, the following act was passed in October, 1782:

AN ACT TO INDEMNIFY CERTAIN PERSONS IN SUPPRESSING A CONSPIRACY AGAINST THIS STATE:

I. WHEREAS divers evil-disposed persons in the year one thousand seven hundred and eighty, formed a conspiracy and did actually attempt to levy war against this commonwealth; and it is represented to the present general assembly, that William Preston, Robert Adams, junior, James Callaway, and Charles Lynch, and other faithful citizens, aided by detachments of volunteers from different parts of the state, did, by timely and effectual measures, suppress such conspiracy: And whereas the measures taken for that purpose may not be strictly warranted by law, although justifiable from the imminence of the danger;

II. BE IT THEREFORE ENACTED, That the said William Preston, Robert Adams, junior, James Callaway, and Charles Lynch, and all other persons whatsoever, concerned in suppressing said conspiracy, or in advising, issuing or executing any orders, or measures taken for that purpose, stand indemnified and exonerated of and from all pains, penalties, prosecutions, actions, suits, and damages on account thereof. And that if any indictment, prosecution, action, or suit shall be laid or brought against them or any of them, for any act or thing done therein, the defendant, or defendants may plead in bar, or in general issue, and give this act in evidence.

And, according to Mr. Page, the proceedings were imitated widely throughout the former colonies and came to be known by the name of Lynch's Law.

To the reader this historical precedent for the vilest of modern practices may seem a bit far-fetched. The legendry of lynching has many more interesting and plausible accounts of its origin, but all of them appear, upon investigation, to be spun of shoddy and other synthetic fabrics unable to bear up under any sort of scrutiny. The story of the patriotic Colonel's activities bears the stamp of authenticity, which the folk tales of the old men and women who "knew him when" do not.

It is a far cry from Lynch's patriotic activities, which gave a new verb to the American language and another personality to our list of legendary characters, to present-day lynch-executions, with their barbarous forms of torture and cruel death and carnivals of sadism. It is a still further cry from the efforts of the original Lynch to maintain order and security in the face of armed invasion to the Judge Lynch of today, who, in a peaceful nation, is a constant menace to the order of our society and the security of more than fifteen millions of our citizens.

Chapter Two

THE EARLY LIFE AND TIMES OF
JUDGE LYNCH

THE career of the legendary Judge Lynch is an American saga. Early in life he took over the office so competently filled by Squire Birch, and performed the duties of the lower court with a promptness and energy that won for him the admiration of his more impatient and energetic fellow-citizens. No untried cases clogged the Judge's docket, there were no postponements or other delays, his decisions were quick and their execution never delayed. There were few appeals from his decisions, and practically no reversals. So effective was his handling of the cases brought before him that when the opportunity presented itself he was elevated to the bench of the Court of Uncommon Pleas, the court from which there is no appeal.

During the early years of the nineteenth century the practice of lynching followed along the traditional lines of flogging and tarring and feathering. In certain cases the sentence was death by flogging or hanging, occasionally by burning. In the succeeding years, the Judge narrowed his decisions to death and sought variety only in a refinement and intensification of the methods of executing the sentence. Before long in his new berth he became known far and wide as "the hanging judge," and his jurisdiction spread across the American continent, confined only by the two oceans and the two borders. Within these confines he rides his circuit, and neither distance nor weather halts his grisly progress.

The earlier work of Judge Lynch was confined to those calls made upon him by the better people of the community to try offenders of public morals, offenders against prevailing social customs, and, on occasion, persons who had committed acts of outrageous criminality. His code was flexible to a degree; invariably the accused was permitted a defense and at times convinced the court of his innocence or was able to show extenuating influences or justification.

There was a period between the surrender of the British at Yorktown and the breakdown of the Crown judicial system and the subsequent development of an American code, based on the various courts. The transition was not accomplished overnight: in the more developed sections it was achieved with a degree of dispatch that made the change almost imperceptible; in the sparsely settled and the newly settled sections it required many years. Courts in some of these places were of limited authority, others did not know how far under a democracy their authority carried and were often arbitrary beyond their powers. In the unsettled communities close to the frontiers, the people were too busy defending themselves from the Indians to worry much about law, and often founded sizable communities that had to depend for their court on some distant county seat.

As the towns prospered and became populated, the lack of a law court, civil and criminal, became evident, and sometimes they awaited long the appointment of a judge or the visits of the circuit justices. In the meantime the people took the law into their own hands and tried the guilty themselves. Lacking jails and the time to transport the accused to distant courthouses for further trial, they resorted to the extra-legal methods of Judge Lynch. Punishment for criminality of all types became corporal; a man was beaten or he was hanged. This type of justice followed the frontier from east to west and continued in existence until the frontier was closed, approximately in the eighteen nineties; yet, as late as 1915 and 1916 we find records of hangings on charges of desperadism in western states.

It is safe to estimate that by the beginning of the nineteenth century, law enforcement and observation were prevalent in all but frontier localities. This period has been termed an era of good feeling, prosperity, and the expansion of industry and markets; we see in it the gradual demand and awarding of more and more democratic processes. No property restrictions to suffrage and the caucus system of selecting candidates for the presidency and vice-presidency were finding adherents throughout the country. Democracy was in full swing, and Andrew Jackson was its high priest and holy prophet.

Democracy's lay-preachers were going up and down the land assuring the people that every man was a king. Everyman was believing it and, looking about him with his royal eye, found much that displeased him. He assumed that it was his kingly prerogative to change the things he didn't like, but his authority, he sadly learned, was confined to his own person and to small local groups who thought as he did. He had never thoroughly learned the theory of democracy and, therefore, was never able to practise it. Where he could not get his way by diplomacy, he brought in force and violence; he had won everything that way, and it seemed the correct way.

The things that displeased everyman were social and economic. He disliked the aliens who were flocking in, particularly the Irish and their church, whom he tried to rout. In the North he joined his southern brothers in disliking the Negro; but he disliked him especially because he was a slave, and slave labor was having an unfavorable effect on the entire country. From the North he loosed upon the South a flood of anti-slavery advocates, most of them self-appointed and self-financed.

The South at first paid little attention to these propagandists, for their efforts were confined almost entirely to the whites, masters of slaves, and to the ministry. It was not until 1829 that David Walker, a free Negro living in Boston, published his pamphlet, *Walker's Appeal*. The author had been born in South Carolina, the son of a free Negress and a slave. He had acquired enough education to read and write, and had come to Boston, where he opened a second-hand clothing store.

The appeal comprised four articles and a preamble addressed to "the Colored Citizens of the World," but, in particular and very expressly, to those of the United States of America. The pamphlet was circulated through the mails at the expense of the author. Copies found their way into the hands of city officials in Atlanta and Richmond and were referred to the Governors of Georgia and Virginia, who in turn submitted them to their respective legislatures.

Official protests were sent to Mayor Otis of Boston, demanding immediate suppression of the subversive booklet. Otis replied that the pamphlet had been written by a free black man, whose true name it bore; that it had not been circulated in Boston; that he did not personally or officially subscribe to its sentiments nor could he prohibit its circulation through the mails. He would, and did, publish a general warning to ship captains and others not to expose themselves to the consequences of carrying the incendiary booklet or other similar writings into the southern states.

The Georgia legislature, not satisfied with the Mayor of Boston's answer, framed and passed a measure providing for forty days' quarantine of all vessels having free Negroes on board, prohibiting intercourse with such vessels by free Negroes or slaves, and making the teaching of free Negroes to read and write a penal offense. In Virginia, at a secret session of the House of Deputies, a bill was passed making it a misdemeanor to teach or permit free Negroes, slaves, or mulattoes to be taught to read or write; it also prescribed fine, imprisonment, *flogging, or death* for any white person, free Negro, slave, or mulatto who should write, print, or circulate among slaves, free Negroes, or mulattoes any paper, book, or pamphlet tending to incite insurrection or rebellion. The bill did not pass the Senate.

In Louisiana, where copies of *Walker's Appeal* had been discovered, the legislature enacted a law forbidding free Negroes to enter the State of Louisiana and commanding all who had entered since 1825 to leave within sixty days.

However, the passing of laws and the death of Walker a year after his pamphlet was published did not stop the flow of anti-slavery literature into the southern states. In 1831, on New Year's day, William Lloyd Garrison issued the first number of what was later to become the most powerful and influential abolitionist weapon, *The Liberator*. Free Negroes gave it their hearty support from the beginning, and by the whites it was attacked and denounced as incendiary and, with *Walker's Appeal*, credited as one of the chief causes of the frightful Southampton massacre.

The southern states were not strangers to Negro or slave revolts. Previous to the Southampton outbreak, Virginia had had seven slave rebellions, South Carolina seven, North Carolina three, Georgia two, and Maryland and Louisiana one each. All of them were suppressed or nipped in the bud, but they served the purpose of keeping the South on its guard. In 1800, Gabriel, a slave belonging to Thomas Prosser, residing near the city of Richmond, made his plans quietly and in secrecy and his revolt was already in motion before it was discovered. Negroes, to the number of eleven hundred, had gathered in the night at a brook some six miles from the city. Under the general leadership of Gabriel they were divided into several divisions, each with an objective: one was to seize the penitentiary, containing several thousand stand of arms; a second was to take the powder house; while the main body was to press on and take the Capitol building, which was to be used as a rallying point and a stronghold. From there on the rebels were to commence the work of slaughter: not a white, save the French inhabitants, was to be spared.

All conditions at first conspired to make the insurrection a success. Richmond was not even in a good defensive position; it would be easy to capture, and, if the objectives were taken, easier to hold. Secrecy stood in Gabriel's favor until the last hour, when, already on the march, the rebels were forced by a swollen stream to stop. The pause gave sufficient time for two slaves to divulge the plot to the white masters and the revolt was put down. Patrols were established in Richmond and surrounding towns; on plantations strict surveillance of Negro quarters was maintained. Arrests, brief hearings, and executions quickly followed, from five to fifteen slaves being hanged at a time. Gabriel eluded arrest, and three hundred dollars was offered for his apprehension. He was later captured in Norfolk, after having lain in a vessel's hold for eleven days, and was hanged on October 7, 1800.

Each executed slave meant a property loss to his owner that was not entirely repaid by the state. As Virginia lands grew less productive and the planters faced a future with limited incomes, breeding slaves for the market gradually assumed the proportions of a leading industry, a matter of some four million dollars annually in the late eighteen fifties. Publicity of the slave revolts would have practically destroyed the market value of Negroes bred in Virginia, and, though there are frequent references to incipient revolts in letters, all public information was suppressed. In 1816 the slaves of Fredericksburg planned a revolt, but the leaders were betrayed and later hanged.

In June, 1822, Charleston, South Carolina, heard rumors of a slave uprising. Denmark Vesey, a free Negro, aided by a Peter Poyas, had enlisted Negroes of from forty to fifty miles about the city in a conspiracy to slaughter the whites and free the blacks. Poyas alone had enlisted no less than six hundred slaves, and it was one of these, a household servant, who revealed the plot to his master. After a month's investigation, only fifty of the thousand supposed to

have been concerned were apprehended. Denmark
Vesey, Peter Poyas, and thirty-three others were put
to death without revealing their secrets.

In 1830 the South wanted the Negro, free and
slave, under control, and the flood of abolitionist
literature, addressed as it was, for the greater part, to
the Negro, was regarded as a menace. Few slaves
could read, but many free Negroes and some slaves
whose masters, through kindness, had given them the
rudiments of education, could and did carry the message of the anti-slavery advocates. The entire South
was frightened; the slaves lived a different life, spoke
almost a different language from their masters; and,
as long as the subversive literature was being circulated, there was no security for the whites. The only
hope of the southern states was to choke it off at the
source.

Each revolt was unsuccessful, yet each one served
to put the Negro farther back in his struggle for
education and independence. The laws enacted by
South Carolina as a result of Denmark Vesey's conspiracy were unusually severe. All persons of color
were debarred from education in its simplest forms;
all free Negroes coming into the state were to be imprisoned. Numbers of colored men, some of them
citizens from the free states, were seized from vessels
in South Carolina ports, imprisoned, and finally sold

into slavery to pay the costs of trial and imprisonment.

The free states, egged on by the abolitionists, protested, and Massachusetts sent the Hon. Samuel Hoar, an eminent attorney, to Charleston to effect and procure the release of several colored men, citizens of the Bay State, imprisoned under this ordinance. Mr. Hoar, accompanied by his daughter, proceeded upon his mission, but was compelled to retire in haste from Charleston under threats of personal violence. No one, black or white man, from a northern state was permitted to enter South Carolina's jurisdiction if he proposed to question the validity of her acts.

Southern ground was being prepared for the advent of Judge Lynch.

The insurrection in Southampton County, Virginia, in August, 1831, was unlike any of the previous slave uprisings in that it was not the result of a carefully elaborated plan. It was the result of one man's inspiration, of a single night's conference in the woods by seven black men who proceeded to the work of slaughter almost as soon it was determined upon and the first steps arranged. Nat Turner, the leader, was, like his predecessors, Gabriel and Vesey, a "good nigger."

On Sunday, August 21, six slaves met in the woods

37

on the plantation of Joseph Travis, ostensibly for a barbecue. The Travis plantation was located in the neighborhood known as Cross Keys, about fifteen miles from Jerusalem Court House and about the same distance from Petersburg. When the roasted pig was ready, the six who had prepared it were joined by a seventh, a dark mulatto in the prime of life, powerfully built, with strongly marked African features and a face indicative of intelligence and resolution. This was Nat Turner.

After the pig was eaten, Turner harangued his fellows in earnest, moving rhetoric depicting the wretchedness of the Negroes' lot and proving by Scripture that he had been called to free his brothers. All conceded the truth of his assumption and declared themselves ready to follow him. The conference continued for several hours.

"It was agreed," said Turner later in his confession, "that we should commence at home that night and, until we had armed and equipped ourselves and gained sufficient force, neither age nor sex was to be spared, which was invariably adhered to." The general design was to conquer Southampton County first and then the rest of the state. In case of defeat they could retreat to the Dismal Swamp, which was about twenty-five miles distant, in whose fastnesses they felt they could find security.

The Negroes left their retreat after midnight, and before dawn were well started on their short career of death and destruction. The house of a widow was first visited, and the family of five whites murdered. A neighbor hearing their screams hurried to the scene to find all five dead; on his return to his own home, he was informed by his Negro houseboy that his own wife and child had been murdered. The family of Turner's master were the next victims, and the leader, with new recruits by dawn, continued his work of slaughter.

In one thing the Negroes were more humane than Indians or white men fighting against Indians: there was no gratuitous outrage beyond the death blow itself, no insult, no mutilation. But in every house they entered the blow fell on men, women, and children; no one with a white skin escaped. From every house they took arms and ammunition, and from a few, money. On every farm and plantation they secured recruits. The mob increased from house to house, first to fifteen, then to forty, finally to sixty-odd. Some were armed with muskets, others with axes and even scythes; some commandeered their dead masters' horses. Before the day closed, fifty-five whites—men, women, and children—had been killed.

The other whites, driven from their homes, abandoned everything in the desire to get away from danger and to shut from their eyes the sight of the vengeful Negroes. Annoyed by the slow progress of his men and realizing that delay would bring armed whites from other districts, Turner decided to strike out for Jerusalem Court House to intercept fugitives and cut off communication with Norfolk and Fortress Monroe. His men, still three miles from the Court House, decided to stop and enlist the many slaves of a Mr. Parker. The halt proved disastrous. Eighteen white men, mounted and armed, rode up and confronted the whole body of blacks. In the pitched battle that followed, the Negroes drove off the whites, pursuing them and killing and wounding several. A fresh band of whites coming up at that moment stayed the pursuit, gave fresh battle, and compelled the blacks to break and run. Those on foot scattered, leaving their leader and about twenty others to fight it out. Turner saw that his cause was lost, that more and more white men were arriving, and gave the order to scatter and seek shelter. A few were told where they were to meet him. The mob dispersed as though into air, many members returning to their homes as though nothing of import had occurred.

Roving bands of armed white men sought out the Negroes; many of the rebellious slaves were shot on sight, and some innocent Negroes suffered. Some prisoners, taken near Cross Keys by troops from Fortress Monroe, were shot and their heads left for weeks stuck on poles as a warning to others who might undertake a similar course. It is alleged that the captain of the marines, on his way back to the barracks, bore the head of a Negro on his sword; it was a good trick, no matter how he managed it. Another revealing story is that of a Negress who attempted to kill her mistress: she was dragged out after she had been taken prisoner, tied to a tree, and her body riddled with bullets. It is said that *some slaves suffered fearful tortures, being burnt with red-hot irons and their bodies being horribly mutilated before death came to their relief.*[1]

The patrols continued for days, destroying every black man they met with. "It was," said a member of the House of Delegates, "with the utmost difficulty and at the hazard of personal popularity and esteem, that the coolest and most judicious among us could exert an influence sufficient to restrain the indiscriminate slaughter of the blacks who were suspected." A letter from a clergyman on the spot said: "There are thousands of troops searching in every direction, and many Negroes are killed every day: the exact number will never be ascertained. Men

[1] Cutler: *Lynch-Law.*

were tortured to death, burned, maimed and subjected to nameless atrocities." [2]

Slave owners, those who had not been destroyed by Turner and his mob, began filing claims for compensation for slaves killed to the number of over one hundred—this, in face of the fact that the widest estimate of Turner's forces gave the number at sixty-odd. Nor was the slaughter of blacks stayed until slave owners threatened to shoot down any "patrol" found on their premises. Not a few of these self-constituted guardians of the peace later boasted that they had killed their "share of the niggers."

Fifty-five slaves were arrested for trial, of whom seventeen were convicted and hanged, twelve transported to the deep south, twenty acquitted, and others held for further examination. Turner evaded capture for six weeks; his retreat was a hole in the ground under a pile of fence rails. When he was taken he was persecuted in various ways, whipped, and sentenced to be hanged. His confession implicated no others, assumed all the blame, and asked the mercy of his God. His body, after death, was turned over to surgeons for dissection. For the benefit of other slaves who might seek freedom through insurrection, the news was broadcast that his skin had been tanned for leather and his body rendered to grease.

[2] Victor: *History of American Conspiracies.*

Despite Turner's confession, there was no doubt in the minds of the Southerners as to who was responsible for Nat Turner's insurrection. As though by universal accord, the accusing fingers of the entire South were pointed in the direction of William Lloyd Garrison, Arthur Tappan, and George Thompson. Copies of their papers were burned and their agents were mobbed and beaten whenever discovered. The insurrection only served to fasten the chains of ignorance more firmly upon the Negro; too, it deprived him of the confidence of his masters, it restricted his little liberties, and substituted violence and cruelty. After that day, for a colored man to be caught conning a spelling book was to bare his back to the lash.

There was a more grievous indictment of the whites than of their rebelling slaves. Where Turner had killed cleanly, the whites in retaliation tortured, mutilated, and burned, conducting themselves like barbarians. In offenses committed by Negroes and Abolitionists, the orderly processes of the law no longer sufficed; the law was too slow.

The education of Judge Lynch was progressing.

The governors of the slave states did nothing to ameliorate conditions. Despite Turner's confession, the Governor of Virginia told the legislature that there was much reason to believe that the insurrection in Southampton and the plots discovered elsewhere had been "designed, planned and matured by unrestrained fanatics in some of the neighboring States, who find facilities in distributing their views and plans amongst our populaton, either through the postoffice, or by agents sent for that purpose throughout our territory."

Other governors of southern states wrote to the executives of the free states from which the incendiary publications had been issued, asking that they be suppressed, or that they at least not be sent into the slave states. Refusal to make use of every possible means to achieve these demands would be evidence of a spirit "hostile to that friendship and good understanding which should characterize sister States." Almost to a man the governors of the offending states pointed out that the writers and publishers were free citizens, that their respective state constitutions upheld the right of free speech and a free press, and that they, regrettably, could do nothing. The people of the South realized, too, that under the law they could do little to prevent the invasion and circulation of abolitionist literature, and they turned to violence and asked the young Judge Lynch to hear some of their cases.

According to Garrison's *The Liberator* of October, 1831, a dispatch dated Wilmington, North Carolina, September 28, said: "Three ringleaders of the late diabolical conspiracy were executed at Onslow Court House on Friday evening last, 23rd instant, by the people." The news was followed by the editor's bitter comment that "executed by the people doubtless means executed by a mob on suspicion of guilt, without investigation or trial."

In what were known as the free states of the North, the abolitionists were no happier than in the slave states. In 1833 a meeting in Clinton Hall, New York City, was called to demand the immediate emancipation of the slaves and the formation of an Anti-Slavery Society. The call had gone out to those sympathetic to the cause, but before it was opened, the hall was taken over by those opposed to the movement. The owners ordered it closed, and the meeting adjourned to Tammany Hall, where resolutions were adopted declaring it improper and inexpedient to agitate the question of slavery and assuring the South of a fixed and unalterable determination to resist every attempt to interfere with the relation of master and slave.

It was during the immediate excitement of this episode that William Lloyd Garrison returned from England, determined to open his great anti-slavery campaign in New York City. He abandoned his intention at once and hurried on to Boston, but word

45

of the Tammany Hall meeting had preceded him, and his arrival was met with an attempt to mob him. A handbill was distributed urging all true Americans to attend the greeting armed with plenty of tar and feathers.

That year Garrison succeeded in forming the American Anti-Slavery Society, with the avowed purpose of organizing subsidiary societies in every city, town, and village in the land, to send forth agents, circulate tracts and pamphlets, enlist the pulpit and press in the cause of the slave, give preference to the products of free labor over those of slaves, and bring the nation to a speedy repentance.

In the southern states the agents were met by mobs and beaten, tarred and feathered, and taken to the city or county line and warned that further offense would be treated more violently. In the North the reaction was against the Negroes, and a mania for Negro-mobbing broke out: there were riots at Columbia and Lancaster, Pennsylvania, Trenton and Bloomfield, New Jersey, and Rochester, New York. In Philadelphia, several persons were killed and others wounded, and thirty houses were destroyed. Investigation showed that the riots were due to the fact that many employers preferred the cheaper black labor and so made it difficult for white working men to support their families. Among other causes were the

46

demonstrations by Negroes whenever a fugitive slave was tried in the courts.

While in England, Garrison had invited George Thompson, a distinguished orator in the cause of abolition in Great Britain, to lecture in America. Thompson arrived in New York in September, 1834. He was greeted by a warning in the *Courier and Enquirer* not to lecture in that city, and was ejected from his suite in the Atlantic Hotel at the demand of an angry Southerner. He then began a lecture tour of New England and fared no better. In Augusta, Maine, the windows of his lodging were stoned and he was requested to leave town under penalty of a mobbing; at Concord his meeting was broken up, and in Lowell he was prevented from speaking by a mob that later adopted a resolution assuring the South that its rights would not be interfered with by the North.

For all these adverse reactions, the Abolitionists went on with their work. In 1835 the American Anti-Slavery Society sent an appeal to the local societies asking for $30,000 for more agents, more literature, and wider distribution. Most of the money was subscribed at once, and twenty-five thousand copies of *The Slave's Friend* and fifty thousand each of *Human Rights*, *Anti-Slavery Record*, and *The Emancipator* were sent into southern states. None was addressed directly to free Negroes or to slaves, though the zealous agents were not instructed to limit their distribution to the whites.

Almost simultaneously with this flood of abolitionist literature into the southern states, two Negroes in Lexington, Mississippi, were overheard talking of a planned insurrection among the slaves. Rumors already afloat indicated that the infamous Murrell gang was planning a revolt of the blacks. The two Negroes were examined at public meeting, and so improbable were their stories that they were remanded to jail to await further developments. A mob immediately formed and, fearing the Negroes would be set free, seized and hanged them.

This was excellent training for young Judge Lynch. Too, it was excellent mob action: the investigation now had to proceed without its two most important witnesses. The mob action continued with the appointment of a vigilance committee vested with full power to arrest, try, condemn, and execute. Two white men, named Cotton and Saunders, itinerant steam doctors by profession, were arrested, placed on trial, and ordered hanged. One, before the noose was tightened, made a confession in which he boasted that he had agents on every plantation and warned the committee to beware of the Fourth of July, naming several black and white confederates. Those named were seized, and some were hanged and others slicked —that is, stripped naked, laid on their stomachs with their hands and feet bound to pegs driven into the ground, and flogged. In all, three white men and an undetermined number of Negroes were hanged *without due process of the law*.

It was in the state of Mississippi that Judge Lynch first mounted the bench, and it is not remarkable that he is still the court of final justice in that state. Since 1882 it has consistently led all the other states in the number of cases it has referred to Judge Lynch, and it has accepted his decision no less than 549 times (December 1, 1937). But the Judge's services were in too great demand to permit him to remain in a single state; a whole section of the country was calling for him. Before he left, however, he took another case in Mississippi.

Vicksburg was long a noted gambling town, harboring a nest of gamblers who had become so powerful that they dominated the political life of the city and terrorized all who were not sympathetic to their activities. During the Fourth of July celebration of 1835, one of the gamblers became so insulting that he was taken into the woods, tied to a tree, flogged, and ordered to leave town within twenty-four hours. The underworld at once showed its teeth, and, before the day's festivities were over, a great mass meeting of indignant citizens was held. "For years past, the gamblers have made our city their place of rendezvous. They support a large number of tippling-houses . . . no citizen is ever secure from their villainy. Our streets are ever resounding with the echoes of their drunken mirth. . . ." [3] A set of resolutions was submitted and adopted by unanimous acclaim:

"Resolved: That notice be given to all professional gamblers, that the citizens of Vicksburg are resolved to exclude them from this place and this vicinity; and that twenty-four hours' notice be given them to leave the place.
"Resolved: That all persons permitting faro-dealing in their houses, be also notified they will be prosecuted therefor.
"Resolved: That 100 copies of the foregoing resolutions be printed and stuck up at the corners of the streets—and that this publication be deemed notice."

Some fifty of the gamblers took heed and fled, but they were the small fry, easily frightened; the top men, the worst characters, remained, and on the night of the fifth, another was taken out and treated like his fellow of the day before. More left, but five remained, and, deciding to give the mob a dose of its own medicine, barricaded themselves in the tavern of John North, ready for anything. On the sixth, the

[3] Coates: *The Outlaw Years.*

mob reassembled and, followed by a crowd of towns-
men, marched to the barricaded gin mill and demanded the unconditional surrender of the gamblers.
This was refused.

The tavern was surrounded, and an effort made to
force an entrance. As the door was burst open, the
gamblers replied with gunfire, and Dr. Hugh S. Bod-
ley went forward to parley. A shot from an upper
window killed him, and the fight was on. Incensed,
the mob rushed into the building and overcame the
gamblers by force of numbers. Five were captured,
including the owner of the tavern, and they were
dragged out, pummeled, and strung up in convenient
doorways along the street. Orders were issued that
their bodies were to hang for twenty-four hours, "as a
warning against those that had escaped." Later the
bodies were cut down and buried in a ditch.

The year 1835, his first on the bench, was a heavy
one for Judge Lynch. His jurisdiction was broaden-
ing and he was being requested to hear cases of all
types, all over the South. Many of the lesser cases
were turned over to Squire Birch. The Judge confined his interests to cases having racial, politico-
economic backgrounds, and those involving religious
controversy. But, he insisted, they must be capital
cases or referred to the lower court of Squire Birch.
Niles' Weekly Register, in its issue of September 5,

1835, commented upon the activities both of Lynch and Birch.

"During the last and present week we have cut out and laid aside more than 500 articles, relating to the various excitements now acting upon the people of the United States, public and private! Society seems everywhere un-hinged, and the demon of 'blood and slaughter' has been let loose upon us! We have the slave question in many different forms, including the proceedings of kidnapers and manstealers—and others belonging to the free Ne-groes: the proscription and persecution of gamblers: with mobs growing out of local matters—and a great col-lection of acts of violence of a private or personal nature, ending in death; and regret to believe, also, that an awful political outcry is about to be raised to rally the 'poor against the rich'! We have executions and murders and riots to the utmost limits of the union. The character of our countrymen seems suddenly changed, and thou-sands interpret the law in their own way—sometimes in one case, and then in another, guided apparently only by their own will."

In that year and in the years immediately follow-ing, Judge Lynch set the pattern for his entire career. Those brought before him were no longer beaten as a punitive measure and sent off; if they were beaten, it was to the death—if they escaped death in that manner, it was to meet it by hanging, drowning, or burning. Only with the aid of inventions, not yet perfected, was the Judge to be able to vary his orders in carrying out the death sentence.

Even before the *Niles' Register* lament had appeared, Judge Lynch had been summoned across the border into the state of Alabama. *The Liberator* of July 4, 1835, reprinted an item from a Mobile paper. Two Negroes were on trial for most barbarously murdering two children, and obviously guilty. "As the Court pronounced the only sentence known to the law . . . the smothered flame broke forth. The laws of the country had never conceived that crimes could be perpetrated with such peculiar circumstances of barbarity, and had therefore provided no adequate punishment. Their lives were justly forfeited to the laws of the country, but the peculiar circumstances demanded that the ordinary punishment should be departed from . . . they were seized, taken to the place where they perpetrated the act, and burned to death."

It might have been 1935; the story would almost read the same. On November 12, 1935, in Colorado, Texas, a mob estimated at seven hundred persons took two Negroes, accused of the murder of a white girl, from the officers of the law and hanged them at the scene of their crime.

Before Judge Lynch had been a year on the bench of the higher court, he had struck his full stride. The earliest of his many *causes célèbres* first came before him for hearing in the spring of 1836, in St. Louis, Missouri, and, though an attempt was made to reverse his decision, it was upheld by none other than—Judge Lawless.

"Greater love hath no man—" . . . the tremendous implications of the words were not meant for colored men, free or slave, black or mulatto. Subsequent to the actions of 1836, no Negro may lift his hand in defense of another Negro, not if the first Negro's opponent is a white man. Too many colored men have stretched hemp for aiding their friends to escape from the law and from the lawless to make exception to this ruling of Judge Lynch.

In April, 1836, a colored man was arrested for some forgotten offense on a Mississippi river boat. A mulatto, a freeman named McIntosh, it was alleged, aided the prisoner to escape and was in turn arrested by the officers. He turned upon the officers, drew a knife, and stabbed a deputy sheriff, killing him instantly, and seriously wounded a constable. McIntosh made his escape, but was later captured and locked up in a St. Louis jail. Later a mob assembled and threatened to tear down the jail if the prisoner was not delivered to it, secured the Negro and conducted him to the outskirts of St. Louis. His body was bound with ropes and fastened to a tree with chains, a few feet from the ground. A fire was then started beneath him and he was roasted to death.

Even in those rough and tough days, this atrocity was too much for the citizens of St. Louis, and the matter was placed before the Grand Jury of St. Louis County for action. Judge Lawless made the following astounding charge:

"I have reflected much on this matter, and after weighing all the considerations that present themselves as bearing upon it, I feel it my duty to state my opinion to be, that whether the Grand Jury shall act at all, depends upon the solution of this preliminary question, namely, whether the destruction of McIntosh was the act of the 'few' or the act of the 'many.'

"If on a calm view of the circumstances attending this dreadful transaction, you shall be of the opinion that it was perpetrated by a definite, and, compared to the population of St. Louis, a small number of individuals, separate from the mass, and evidently taking upon themselves, as contradistinguished from the multitude, the responsibility of the act, my opinion is that you ought to indict them all, without a single exception.

"If on the other hand, the destruction of the murderer of Hammond was the act as I have said, of the many—of the multitude, in the ordinary sense of those words—not the act of numerable and ascertainable malefactors, but of congregated thousands, seized upon and impelled by that mysterious, metaphysical and almost electric phrensy, which, in all nations and ages, has hurried on the infuriated multitude to deeds of death and destruction—then I say, act not at all in the matter—the case transcends your jurisdiction—it is beyond the reach of human law."

Which seems as nice a bit of judicial fence-straddling as one could hope to find in a lifetime's search. What Judge Lawless—his tribe has increased—meant was that if two or three do the lynching, it is indefensible, but that if it is perpetrated by a number, uncountable at a glance or undeterminable in the night, it is all right. To avoid prosecution in the future, mobs must be bigger and better, at least "many." As travel conditions improved, the Judge believed, he would be able to command mobs numbering more than ten thousand.

The case was not yet finished. For denouncing the burning of McIntosh and violently attacking the decision of Judge Lawless in his weekly paper, *The Observer*, The Reverend Elijah F. Lovejoy had his printing office destroyed by the mob. The press, however, was saved and shipped twenty-five miles up the Mississippi to Alton, Illinois, where Lovejoy planned to set it up and resume publication. But the mob took it from the wharf and dumped it into the river the night it arrived. Alton people, led by the Presbyterians, held a mass meeting, denounced the action of the mob, and subscribed money for a new press. Lovejoy started *The Alton Observer* with the statement:

"As long as I am an American I shall hold myself at liberty to speak, to write, and to publish whatever I please on any subject, being amenable to the laws of my country for the same."

He continued his attacks on slavery and lynching and, in July, 1837, the mob again destroyed his printing equipment. A third press was ordered, and when it arrived the mob broke it up and threw the pieces into the Mississippi. Lovejoy's friends were with him; they rallied, and a fourth press was ordered. At three in the morning the river boat carrying it made fast to the wharf and fifty men escorted the press to the stone warehouse. A small mob hooted, blew horns, and threw stones, but the precious machine was delivered in safety and a guard placed over it.

That night the mob re-formed and demanded that the press be delivered to them for destruction; when this demand was refused, they hurled stones through the windows. Then a gun was fired and other shots followed. One of the defenders of the press fired his piece and killed a man in the mob. The assailants withdrew for a time but returned with ladders, which were placed against the building, and an attempt was made to fire the roof. When Lovejoy and a few of his

57

supporters tried to prevent this, the clergyman received five shots in his body and died a few minutes later. The men guarding the press, seeing their leader down, beat a hasty retreat, and the mob entered the warehouse unresisted and threw the offending press from the windows. The work of destruction was finished with sledge hammers by the mob in the street.

There was yet another voice raised against Judge Lynch. A young lawyer of twenty-eight arose before the Young Men's Lyceum of Springfield, Illinois, on the night of January 27, 1837, to deliver an address on "The Perpetuation of Our Political Institutions." Abraham Lincoln, speaking before Lovejoy's death, said, in part:

"Accounts of outrages committed by mobs form the everyday news of the times. They have pervaded the country from New England to Louisiana. . . . It would be tedious as well as useless to recount the horrors of all of them. Those happenings in the State of Mississippi and at St. Louis are perhaps the most dangerous in example and revolting to humanity. In the Mississippi case they first commenced by hanging the regular gamblers. . . . Next, Negroes suspected of conspiring to raise an insurrection were caught up and hanged in all parts of the State; then, white men supposed to be in league with the Negroes; and, finally, strangers from neighboring states, going

58

thither on business, were in many instances subjected to the same fate. Thus went on the process of hanging, from gamblers to Negroes, from Negroes to white citizens, and from these to strangers, till dead men were literally dangling from the boughs of trees by every roadside. . . . Turn then to that horror-striking scene at St. Louis. A single victim was sacrificed there. . . . A mulatto man by the name of McIntosh was seized in the street, dragged to the suburbs of the city, chained to a tree, and actually burned to death; and all within a single hour from the time he had been a freeman attending to his own business and at peace with the world.

"Such are the effects of mob law, and such are the scenes becoming more and more frequent in this land so lately famed for love of law and order, and the stories of which have now grown too familiar to attract anything more than an idle remark."

In Alton the Grand Jury brought in indictments against several men involved in the slaying of the Reverend Elijah Lovejoy, but the cases were not pressed. When the case of one of the assailants came up in the municipal court, the jury considered him guilty of all the charges but returned a verdict of not guilty on a question of jurisdiction.

Judge Lynch for a time stuck pretty close to the cotton states. He found them fertile fields for his peculiar type of justice and, in those early days, he was but little concerned with the complexion of his victim's skin. In Louisiana a white man killed another white man, and the murderer was tried in a summary manner and executed by hanging. In 1839 two alleged white murderers who had escaped from jail were retaken and remanded to jail to await the collection of testimony; the mob was impatient and, without awaiting the trial, condemned the pair out of hand and hanged them.

Cutler reprints from *Niles' Register* of August 24, 1844:

"Four men, Rea, Mitchell, White and Jones were tried and condemned before his honor, Chief Justice Lynch, on the 16th inst. at South Sulphur, Texas, for killing two men and one boy of the Delaware tribe of friendly Indians. They were executed under said sentence the next day, in the presence of a large number of persons."

In 1845 the Judge was back in Missouri where, in September, he hanged without further trial two white men on the charge of murder. Early the following year he introduced his system of jurisprudence into Florida, and he had to stretch matters to make a go of it.

"A man by the name of Yeoman, accused of being a noted slave stealer, having been discharged by Judge

Warren of Baker County, Georgia, on a writ of *habeas corpus* . . . on his arrival at Jefferson County, Florida, ninety citizens assembled and took a formal vote, which stood 67 for and 23 against hanging him. He was hanged accordingly." [4]

In 1855 Judge Lynch added Tennessee to his list with a mass-hanging of Negroes; a year later he invaded Virginia, but the Old Dominion victim got off with a slicking. In all the slave states, Abolitionists, when caught, were slicked without further ado, and it was only upon occasion that they were put to death. Slaves accused of almost any kind of criminality were transported, and as a rule only free Negroes were put to death. When a slave was destroyed by the mob, the state or the community invariably reimbursed the owner for his loss.

By 1860, lynchings had disgraced every one of the slave states and many of the free states; the fruit of Judge Lynch's decisions hung from many trees. As though bored with simple hangings, and even burnings, the Judge regularly increased the barbarity and savagery of the punishments. They began with whipping, went on to mutilation and half-hanging to burning. Today, as in the case Claude Neal, it is not infrequent for the victim to be slowly hoisted by the neck and then lowered just before death comes to his

[4] *Niles' Weekly Register*, January 17, 1846, quoted by Cutler.

relief and for the torture to be repeated until the lynchers weary of their sadism and mercifully—if the term be permitted in such an instance—kill. The practice of increasing the severity of the punishment continued through the years until, in 1937, a Mississippi mob brought in an entirely new development of torture.

The Liberator of September 14, 1880, printed an extract from a letter written from Houston, Texas. It voices a general Southern complaint.

"Tell your abolition friends to go on and soon they will have the pleasure of seeing the Negro reduced to such a state of hopeless bondage that they may well pity them. I solemnly declare that today the Negro is not as free as he was two or five years ago; and why? Simply because his master has been goaded on to desperation by incendiary acts and speeches. Now he fears the Negro and binds him down as you would a savage animal. One year ago all was peace and quietness here. The Negro was allowed to go out, to have dances and frolics; today one dare not show his head after nine o'clock in the evening. Seven companies of patrols are organized and guard the city each night, sixteen horse-patrol scour the country around. Forty-eight vigilance men say live, banish or die, as the proof may go to show. . . . Men are hung every day by the decision of the planters, lawyers, judges and ministers. It is no hot impetuous act, but cool, stern justice."

Three years before, *The Liberator* reported that a traveler in Texas had seen twelve bodies hanging from one tree and five from another. Editorially, Garrison had said in 1856:

"A record of the cases of 'Lynch Law' in the Southern States reveals the startling fact that within twenty years, over three hundred white persons have been murdered upon the accusation—in most cases unsupported by legal proof—of carrying among slaveholders arguments addressed expressly to their own intellects and consciences, as to the morality and expediency of slavery."

It would be difficult to estimate the number of Negroes lynched in the same twenty years, and it is possible that any estimate based on the few known cases would show that number was considerably less than that for the whites. As has been pointed out, the Negro was property, each adult male of under forty-five being worth approximately $1,500, more if he knew a trade, less if he was "a bad nigger." Garrison's statement cannot be questioned, for most of the white men lynched had been sent to the tasks, to the work that earned for them the death they received at the hands of the mob, by the American Anti-Slavery Society and its branches. Few of the white men were offered the indignities to which the Negroes were subjected; they were politely hanged and their bodies left for the coroner to bury. Savagery and brutality were reserved for the blacks; even after death their bodies were further subjected to mortification. Even in those days, before the Civil War, the lynching of colored people meant more than reprisals for crimes committed, than measures taken to keep the Negro in his place, to protect white womanhood.

Judge Lynch went to California long before gold was discovered. His first recorded case was in San Diego, a city now ill-famed for its tendency to mob action in matters concerned with labor. Like so many subsequent Golden State lynchings, it was a jail snatch.

On the night of March 26, 1833, Antonio Alipas, a private in the presidial company of Loreto, was in the guardhouse for an unrecorded offense. During the evening a corporal and his squad, all mounted and armed, rode up to the jail and demanded that the sergeant deliver Antonio to them. The sergeant refused, and the soldiers forced the guardhouse and took the prisoner for California's first lynching.

Four years later, in Los Angeles, another snatch occurred. Domingo Feliz, a poor but honest cuckold, was murdered by his wife's paramour, Gervasio, aided and abetted by the woman. Gervasio and Maria del Rosario were duly arrested and incarcerated in the local jail. Before they could be brought for trial, a mob assembled, but decided that death was too good for the pair, and returned to their homes. When the funeral of Feliz took place, public clamor demanded the blood of the guilty pair, but Holy Week was at hand and the impetuous demand was postponed until the day after Easter. On Easter Monday it rained and public enthusiasm for the lynching was dampened, and it was put off until the California climate should improve. On Tuesday another postponement threatened when it was found there was no priest available to hear the last confessions of the two sinners. But public clamor could no longer be stilled, and at four-thirty in the afternoon Gervasio was hauled out of jail and shot. After him came the woman, and California gets credit for the first recorded lynching of a woman.[5]

Vigilance as it was conceived was not lynch-law. The discovery of gold in California in 1848, the change from Spanish law to the absence of American law, the indecision about what form of government would prevail, and the corruption after the territory had been admitted to the Union in 1850 all combined to make California a place to be avoided by the peace-

[5] Bancroft: *Popular Tribunals.*

loving. The stampede to the gold fields included men of the highest types and those whose departure from their accustomed haunts brought sighs of content from local peace officers. Once in the mines, the search for the metal occupied the minds and efforts of all, each man using the talents at his command to get rich as quickly as possible. Americans competed with Russians, Frenchmen, Spanish-Americans, and others whose language they did not understand, with criminals from Australia and South America, whose ways they but partially understood.

The Americans protested that these foreigners were being permitted to dig American wealth from American soil and take it, without hindrance, to their own countries. The cry that "the greasers must go" was heard throughout the mines, and a law was passed, the Foreign Miners License Tax, requiring all South Americans to pay twenty dollars monthly for permission to dig for gold. It drove them from the mines into the towns, and their places were taken by Chinese and Pacific Islanders as employees. Later the China Boys and the Kanakas were driven from the mines to the settlements and, added to the natural accretion of a criminal element, made Sacramento and San Francisco nests of crime and criminals.

The absence of strong governments in the cities made criminal activities a profitable venture. Gangs preyed upon merchants and restaurateurs, and when a miner came down from the hills, his poke well-filled with gold, he too became the prey of the vultures. Men of respectability were so absorbed in the accumulation of wealth they could not spare the time for civic activities. When conditions got so bad that they themselves were in danger, they turned and found that the criminal element had completely taken over the local governments. In 1851 they turned to vigilance and effected a superficial and temporary reformation. That the committees made errors, that at times the wrong man was executed, cannot be denied. Even the most firmly established courts err and learn of their mistakes too late for correction.

Like the kangaroo courts of Judge Lynch, the Vigilantes superseded the offices held by the regularly constituted police and peace officers as well as the judiciary. They apprehended the accused, tried him and sentenced him, and, if necessary, executed the duties of the hangman. Considering their success in stamping out criminality, it is difficult to condemn them; they did not take to the execution of summary justice until formal justice had broken down.

Vigilance pursued its way through the West. All the coast states and most of the mountain states sought in it peace and protection of life and property. When the people had stamped out criminality, they returned to their gold-grubbing, ignoring the old adage. The criminals lost no time in returning to their old haunts, and again in 1885 vigilance was called upon to rid the communities of their presence. This time it was stronger, it was more complete and effective, and, when its first tasks were complete, it went on to the polls and elected officials who could be trusted, a judiciary that could not be easily tampered with. The new form, radical and permanent, was adopted throughout the West and, in too many places, became common lynching. Men suspected of crime, others accused of criminal activities, some of them already in the hands of the law, were taken by pseudo-vigilance committees and put to death.

Hangings became spectacles; the condemned were forced to build the scaffolds from which they were later hanged. Men and women came great distances to witness the executions of five, ten, and even twenty robbers and murderers (Idaho). *The New York Times*, on March 19, 1864, commenting upon the activities of the Vigilance Committees throughout the mineral territories, said they "are holding Lynch courts in extraordinary number, and carrying out the decrees of that ferocious judge with unprecedented energy." The same editorial mentions that bills had been passed in Congress enabling Nevada and two other territories to form constitutions preparatory to their admission as states. A condition of admission was an irrevocable ordinance prohibiting slavery, and the writer added: "we think lynching might have been included."

Horse thieves, murderers, and desperadoes have been hanged under the guise of vigilance as late as 1915 in Arizona, when two alleged bandits were lynched at Lonely Gulch; in Texas in 1915, at San Benito, when six were hanged on charges of murder and desperadism; and in Arkansas in 1916 for highway robbery.

The War Between the States did not interrupt the activities of the Vigilance Committees operating in the western territories, but it did change, to some degree, the Southerner's relation to the Negro. After the surrender of General Lee, the Thirteenth Amendment became effective in the former slave states; the slave was now free, but he was still a Negro, still ignorant, still loyal in many cases to his former master. Governor Walker of Florida said in his inaugural address:

"Not only in peace but in war they have been faithful to us. Our women and infant children were left almost exclusively to the protection of our slaves and they proved true to their trust. Not one case of insult,

69

outrage, indignity has come to my knowledge. They remained at home. They raised food for our armies. We know many were anxious to take up arms in our cause. For several years along six hundred miles of coast they heard the guns of Federal ships of war, yet not a thousand of them left our service to find shelter and freedom under the Union flag."

On the other hand, the former slave states began to enact repressive laws barring the free Negro from the expression of his rights. Despite the words of the Governor, Florida would give her assent to the Thirteenth Amendment only with the understanding that no power was given Congress to legislate on "the political status of freedmen in this State." Emancipation having been forced upon the southern states, they, in retaliation and without delay, enacted apprentice acts, vagrancy laws, black codes to define the economic rights of the colored people. To the people of the South the freed Negro differed in no way from the plantation slave, except that he could not be bought and sold, he must be paid for his labor. The sweeping Reconstruction policies of the triumphant North, aimed at changing the whole fabric of a civilization almost overnight, brought about something like chaos in many places. As a result, color lines were drawn with added sharpness, and only such laws for the whites as could with safety, from the Southerner's point of view, be extended to the blacks were enacted in the Negro's favor.

He could not serve in the militia, or sit in a jury box, or testify in court in civil suits unless he was a party to the record, or in criminal actions unless all parties were Negroes or if the culprit before justice was a white man charged with some act of violence to a Negro. He could not carry firearms without a permit, nor ride in a railroad car with white passengers. He could not rent or lease land or houses save in segregated areas set aside by whites. All contracts for labor, if for longer than a month, must be in writing and attested and read to the Negro by a city or county officer or two disinterested whites. Should a Negro run away from his employer, any person might arrest him and bring him back and receive five dollars plus ten cents a mile for doing so. Negro children under eighteen who were orphans, or whose parents refused to support them, must be apprenticed to some suitable person. Freedmen over eighteen who, on the second Monday in January, 1866, had no lawful employment were to be treated as vagrants and fined fifty dollars. If they did not pay, they were to be hired out to any who would pay the fine and costs for the shortest times.[6]

[6] Laws of Mississippi, 1865. Quoted from McMaster: *History of the People of the United States During Lincoln's Administration.*

The state of Mississippi enacted such laws, and, although they were promptly set aside by the Freedmen's Bureau, many were later re-incorporated into the state codes and prevail today in most of the southern states.

With repressive laws ruthlessly set aside by the Freedmen's Bureau, it was necessary for the southern states to call for mob action against any attempt of the Negro to assert his new-found freedom. The Ku Klux Klan may have been started as a social club with no idea of anything but good clean entertainment for its members. When men pull masks over their faces for anything but a masquerade, they are encroaching upon the practices of those engaged in criminal activity. The original Klan called itself a social organization, but its conception of society was terrorizing Negroes. The newly freed Negro was, as a rule, ignorant as a child, often stupid, and as superstitious as any of his race who remained in Africa. The weird Klansmen riding about in hoods and nightshirts did make the night hideous for him for a time. But the average Negro learned quickly that there was nothing to fear from their simple appearance, and the Klan, to continue its work effectively, added whippings and lashing, later hangings and burnings, to its repertory of repressive measures. For a few years it flared across the darkened southern skies, terrorizing black and white alike, until the Government had to put it down forcibly.

But the Southerners who despised the Negro, who feared him, had learned a valuable lesson. Masks, horses, and a sudden foray into the night left no eye-witness who could prove recognition, no accusing fingers. They achieved in an instant the pseudo-reforms they desired, they wreaked vengeance without fear of reprisal. When the Klan was demobilized, it was almost a national or, at least, a sectional institution, and the local units, realizing their powers as a weapon of repression, continued to meet secretly. They called themselves by different names: the White Camelia, Whitecaps, Night-riders, Regulators, etc. The Klan did not need an organization; as such, it merely reflected a type of mentality that prevailed and would continue to prevail no matter what laws were passed. That mentality still prevails, and, whether the resurrected Klan of today thrives or fails as an organization, the hysterical appeals to uphold white supremacy and to protect American womanhood will produce the mob action required.

The dispersion of the Klan in March, 1869, did not stop the activities charged against the organization, and "Ku Klux outrages" continued to be reported in the papers. Coupled with executions by lynch-law on the frontier, the totals for the entire country must have been high. James Elbert Cutler, in his *Lynch-Law*, reports that he turned to the files of *The New York Times* for the three years, 1871–1873, and compiled the following statistics. It will be noted that the Klan, then legally dead for more than two years, is still mentioned.

KENTUCKY: 2 Negroes hanged for rape, 1 white man hanged for rape, 1 Negro hanged for murder, 3 Negroes shot by masked men, 1 Negro "murdered" by the Klan.
TENNESSEE: 2 Negroes hanged for robbery and arson, 1 Negro shot and hanged for robbery and murder, 1 Negro shot for attempted outrage, 1 Negro hanged and shot for murder, 1 white man shot for murder of wife.
MISSOURI: 5 horse thieves hanged, 1 Negro hanged for outrage, 1 white hanged for murder, 3 whites hanged for murder and robbery, 3 whites shot for defending and being bondsmen of county officials accused of peculation.
CALIFORNIA: 2 whites hanged for murder, 1 white hanged and shot for murder, 1 Indian hanged for murder, 1 Malay (steward of steamer) shot and thrown overboard for ravishing sick girl, eleven years old.
MONTANA: 2 whites hanged for murder.
LOUISIANA: 4 Negroes hanged for murder, 3 horse thieves hanged.
VIRGINIA: 1 desperado, horse thief and murderer hanged.
ALABAMA: 1 white shot for murder.
SOUTH CAROLINA: 2 whites shot for murder, 10 Negroes shot and hanged by the Ku Klux Klan.

NEVADA: 1 desperado hanged, 1 white man hanged for murder.

WISCONSIN: 1 white hanged for murder.

INDIANA: 3 Negroes hanged for murder, 1 desperado and 1 horse thief "killed in jail."

NEBRASKA: 1 Negro and 1 white "killed" for robbery and shooting woman.

KANSAS: 2 whites hanged for murder, 1 desperado and 1 horse thief "killed in jail."

COLORADO: 2 whites hanged for keeping gambling outfits.

MICHIGAN: 2 whites died from beating they received for killing a man in a German-Irish riot on the streets.

OHIO: 2 whites hanged for murder.

MARYLAND: 1 Negro hanged for arson.

Total: 41 whites, 32 Negroes, 1 Malay, 1 Indian.

"The majority of those lynched," says Dr. Cutler, "were forcibly taken from officers of the law. In some instances, the jails were broken into, and the prisoners were taken out and hanged or were killed in the jail; in other instances, the prisoners were taken from the officers and put to death before they could be taken to the jail. Some of the lynchings were carried on by vigilance societies, others by mobs of masked persons or by Ku-Kluxes."

These statistics, compiled from a single newspaper, represent only a small percentage of the persons lynched in those years. The total given for three years is only seventy-five, and in 1882, the first year that a comprehensive effort was made to compile a lynch record, we have reported a total of 114 lynch-executions, both white and black.

By 1882 the kangaroo court of Judge Lynch was firmly established throughout the Union; his juris-diction was limited only by the reaches of our own states and territories; his code, or body of laws, was all-embracing, covering every offense from murder down to the thumbing-of-the-nose (Negro to white) and merely being unpopular.

Chapter Three

JUDGE LYNCH'S CODE

To attempt to codify the great body of offenses coming within the purview of Judge Lynch's activities is almost impossible, and the result would be useless. The formal rules of procedure are dispensed with, his advocates do not have to pass any rigorous examinations before they may practise, and precedents set by other cases seldom have any bearing on the one being heard. The usual crimes against person and property head the list, but they share their places with many other offenses, many of which are not recognized in the conventional civil and criminal codes of the land.

One needs only to be suspected or accused of a crime to be dragged before Judge Lynch; the trials are quick, the defendant is never given a chance to defend himself, nor to summon witnesses in his own defense or even hear the charge against him. In moments of great benevolence the Judge will permit the prisoner to plead guilty. Many times the stating of the charge would be unnecessary; the prisoner has heard it in the lower court, proven his innocence, and been acquitted. In too many cases to number the Judge has reversed the lower courts, placed the prisoner in double jeopardy, and, entirely ignoring the first judge, determined the prisoner guilty. Jack West, Negro, of Seminole County, Florida, was such a one. West was acquitted of the charge of breaking and entering and of an assault on a white child. As he was returning to his home, happily proven innocent of the charges, Judge Lynch snatched him from the train and lynched him beside the tracks.

"Not turning out of the road for white boy in auto"; "insulting white man"; "activities in politics"; "demanding pay for work done"; "being brother of a murderer"; "too prosperous"; "too uppity"; "remaining in town where Negroes are not permitted after sunset"—these are capital offenses in Judge Lynch's court.

Often when the Judge's advocates can find no charge against a victim, they convict him of "suspicion of rape" or "suspicion of murder," even when no assaulted girl is to be found and no corpus delicti can be produced. Great numbers of white and black men have been lynch-executed for no better reason than that they were trying to improve the conditions of their fellows and themselves. The spectacle of a worker trying to organize a union, of a sharecropper going among his fellows seeking to improve their working conditions, of a Negro refusing to remain in peonage or not caring to pick cotton, when there is cotton in need of picking, sends the hanging judge into a fury.

Murder, rape, assault, arson, theft, desperadism, and a wildly assorted list of minor offenses are what usually call forth summary action from Judge Lynch, but there are also the categories "cause unknown," "by accident," "without cause," and "mistaken identity."

Of the seven major causes:

Murder includes attempted murder, murderous assault, assault with intent to kill, suspected murder, suspicion of murder, alleged murder, accessory to murder, conspiracy to murder, complicity in murder.

Rape includes attempted rape, suspicion of rape, alleged rape, aiding and abetting a rapist.

Assault is usually connected with murder and rape and includes assault with intent to kill, assault with intent to rape. By itself it includes common assault, assault with intent to rob.

Theft includes breaking and entering, larceny, burglary, robbery, suspected and alleged robbery, cattle, mule, and horse stealing.

Arson includes incendiarism, barn and house burning, haystack burning.

Desperadism includes outlawry, highway robbery,

train robbery or wrecking—in general, the action of a desperado.

Minor offenses are multitudinous and sometimes unbelievable. They differ for blacks and whites. For instance, in the case of miscegenation, it is only the male black who is punished. Those minor offenses for which only whites are punished by lynching are wife-beating, cruelty, kidnaping, seduction, incest; no Negroes are lynched for these offenses as long as they are committed against members of their own race. Among the many offenses that apply to colored offenders are these:

Turning state's evidence, and refusing to turn state's evidence.

Testifying against a white man.

Insulting a white man.

Informing on a white man.

Writing insulting letters to a white man.

Writing any kind of letter to a white woman.

Slandering a white man.

Asking white woman in marriage.

Paying attention to a white girl.

Forcing white boy to commit crime.

Refusing to give right of way to white persons.

Riding in train with white passengers.

Trying to act like a white man.

Other minor offenses are grave robbery; slander;

self-defense; cutting levees; voodooism; poisoning
horses, mules, cattle, and swine; incendiary language;
swindling; colonizing negroes; gambling; quarreling;
throwing stones; poisoning wells; making threats; being troublesome; bad reputation; drunkenness; entic-
ing a servant away; fraud; strike rioting and strike
participation; rioting; conspiracy; introducing small-
pox; conjuring; concealing and aiding criminals to
escape; passing counterfeit money; disobeying ferry
regulations; resisting assault; testifying by a Negro
for another Negro; lawlessness; circulating radical
literature; being found under bed in white man's
house; jumping labor contract; insanity; being a rela-
tive of a man already lynched; peeping in white girl's
window; not stopping an auto when ordered; organizing share-croppers; insulting colored girl; and being
unpopular.

After the Armistice, many Negroes came home
who had served in the Army and Navy and learned,
in the limited freedom given them in the armed services of the country in wartime, that their manhood
was what they themselves made it; that a "good nigger" was the Negro who could take care of himself,
hold up his end, in any company. When they returned to their homes in the South, they sought to
practise their new lesson, and, as a result, within the
first year of the peace, ten Negro veterans, some still

in their uniforms, were lynch-executed in five southern states.[1] How many other Negro heroes were
killed, how many were beaten and barely escaped
with their lives is not in the record. "Frenchwomen-
spoiled niggers," the South called them, another way
of expressing its fear.

If the reader has persevered and read through this
amazing list of offenses for which his fellow-citizens
have paid with their lives, does he recall how many
times he has merited lynching? Let him take heart;
few of the persons lynched were destroyed for the
particular offenses cited. These were but the sparks
that lighted already smoldering prejudices.

The Negro is almost consistently the principal per-
former in American lynch-executions, the victim who
can no longer state his case before any earthly court.
But seldom does he pull the rope, never in any recorded case has he lighted the faggots. In 1908, at Pine
Level, Johnston County, North Carolina, it is recorded that an unnamed Negro entertainer was
lynched by Negroes for putting on a poor show, and
it is within the bounds of probability that all were
drunk; many white performers have felt the ire of
their cheated audiences. In 1934, at Caddo Parish,

[1] Alabama, 1; Arkansas, 2; Florida, 1; Georgia, 3; Mississippi, 3.

Louisiana, Grafton Page, a thirty-year-old Negro, was beaten to death by members of his own race because of an alleged insult offered by Page to a colored girl who had been out driving with him.

One of Judge Lynch's most severe reversals was when Negroes, at Clarksdale, Tennessee, in 1914, lynched a white youth for the rape of a Negress. The coroner's jury, believe it or not, brought in a verdict of justifiable homicide and freed the blacks.

Chapter Four

JUDGE LYNCH'S JURORS

"He who is not against me, is with me."
—JUDGE LYNCH.

WE can dismiss as absurd the contention that lynchings take place only in the backwoods and rural districts of the South. Climate and section do not make for lynch-executions any more than does the lack of theatres or motion picture houses, merry-go-rounds, and symphonic orchestras. There are few places within the territorial United States where it is impossible to rouse a lynch-minded mob, even though it may be frustrated by effective police action. The mob is lying dormant and needs but the spark of an overt act to bring it into snarling action, whether it be in Jacksonville, Florida, San Jose, California, or Duluth, Minnesota. Since the Armistice, lynchings have been prevented in New Hampshire, New York City, and the District of Columbia.

Nor are Judge Lynch's jurors confined to a single class or economic group. The man who pulls the rope or strikes the match is no more guilty of murder than the police officer who refuses to arrest him, the prosecuting attorney who refuses to seek an indictment, the Judge who refuses to convict him; or than those sheriffs and deputies, wardens and jailers, and guards who, brazenly or with a false play at resistance, release their prisoners to the death mobs. Add to these those who commit the crime of refusing to recognize or of denying recognition of members of the lynch mob; those mayors and governors who refuse to call out their state troops to protect one or more of their citizens; and those coroners whose stereotyped verdict that "the deceased came to his death at the hands of persons unknown" is given in the face of criminal knowledge of the actual participants in the murder. The guilt reaches to those representatives of the people who sit in state legislatures or in Congress at Washington and vote against proposed laws to help abolish the crime of lynching.

When the Hanging Judge cries "guilty as charged" and utters the sentence of death, it is the jurors, the mob, who determine the method by which the sentence is to be carried out. Americans who but a few hours before were going about their usual tasks, simple or intricate, become a blood-lusting mob, exercising their imaginations to think up new and more hideous tortures. Shrieking and dancing, men, women, and little children go out to kill or to look on sympathetically while others kill, indulging in practices that would make savages blush.

These are not the lawless elements; nor are they irresponsible mobs, no victory of the lawless over the law. The mob is you and me, and every other American.

Mobs are created; they are man made and man led; they are not the result of spontaneous action, of a sudden uprising of public indignation or community sense of outrage. Mobs have been persistent, suffering several frustrations, only to return weeks later to achieve their determined purpose. Lynch mobs are more baffling than other types of mobs: they seem not content with the punishment of real or alleged offenders, but wish to wreak upon their bodies, both before and after death, greater and more horrible humiliations.

The usual lynch mob is made up of three component parts:

(a) the leaders, who instigate the lynching;

(b) the lynchers, who perform the lynching;

(c) the spectator mob, which encourages the lynchers.

The mob leaders are often, as a matter of record,

men of some local importance, of substance and reputation, prosperous business men and merchants; sometimes they are leading churchmen; and in instances
women have been numbered among the leaders. Most
often they are local and petty politicians, men of easy
living, good fellows who seem to achieve an excellent
standard of living with no great amount of mental
or physical effort. Often, especially in the South, they
are employing farmers, planters, and landlords. Still
in the South, they are likely to be members of the
Democratic party, of either the Baptist or the Meth-
odist Church; they believe the Klan was, and still is,
a good idea—real Americanism, that every Negro's
crowning ambition is to rape a white woman, and
that Negroes can be kept in their place only by occasional warnings in the form of lynch-executions.
The southern mob leader also detests Catholics, labor
leaders, and most Northerners, especially those who
believe the Negro is entitled to the same rights as the
whites. In the North the mob leader may belong to
either major political party, he seldom sees the inside
of a church, and, though he belongs to no repressive
clans, he is in entire sympathy with them. He, too,
hates labor leaders, Communists, "wops," "kikes." In
the West he follows the general pattern, and his added
hates are Japanese, Mexicans, and Filipinos.

The mob leaders, one or more of them, have what

can be called a working agreement with the Sheriff or other officer who has the person of the proposed victim. By working agreement is meant that the leaders have definite knowledge or assurance of the officer's sympathy with their intent; that one or more of the leaders have "something on" the officer; that they know him to be a coward and a craven; or that, because he is seeking political advancement or re-election, he will not offer any militant opposition.

On the part of the officers this working agreement may take the form, as it has in certain instances, of delivering in advance the keys to the jail; of informing the leaders of the proposed route over which the prisoner is to be transported; of placing the prisoner in charge of deputies acquiescent in the will of the mob or willing to be overpowered. Invariably the mob leaders have enough information to determine the weakest link in the police chain. The snatch is made en route to or from the jail, in the jail, at the entrance to the courthouse, or in the courtroom it-self. The snatch completed, the victim is hurried to the place of the proposed execution and delivered or released into the hands of the lynch mob.

The lynch mob is, as a rule, made up of young men between their teens and their middle twenties, with a sprinkling of morons of all ages. Its members are native whites, mostly the underprivileged, the unemployed, the dispossessed, and the unattached. Few of them have completed high school studies, none of them can be classified as adult. They are grocery clerks, soda-jerkers, low-paid employees in jobs that require neither training nor intelligence; jobs that might often be filled more competently by Negroes and at lower wages. In rural communities this mob is made up of day-workers and wage-hands, the more shiftless type of tenants, those who through birth and former position are bound to the locality. The hobo or itinerant worker is seldom a mob member.

The lynch mob, recruited in pool halls and beer parlors, is egged on by the leaders and encouraged by the spectator mob. Its members give full expression to the defeated lusts, to the savage bestiality that was engendered in their hangouts. In their defeated imaginations they believe, during the progress of the lynch-execution, that they are doing a public service, that they have at last taken their place alongside the leaders. They sense the envy and the approval of the spectator mob whose members, in the natural course of local affairs, regarded them as loafers and bums. It is a foul moment, bringing all classes and types together in a sort of vicious brotherhood.

The spectator mob does not actively participate in the lynching, though at times the lynch mob will permit members to take part in protracted bestialities, before and after the death. Its chief purpose is by its presence and voice to lend encouragement to the actual lynchers and to urge them on to greater and more fiendish actions. Like spectators at a baseball game or boxing exhibition, its members shout their personal instructions, urging speed or demanding that those in front sit down. They chant "burn that nigger" and sing that happy days are here again.

This mob is composed largely of men in their thirties and women in their forties. Many, though they do not approve lynching in general, are held in a strange and morbid enchantment, unable to tear themselves away from the sight they will spend years in trying to forget, unwilling to lift their voices in protest or to shut their eyes to the horror.

One thing all three parts of the mob hold in common is the willingness to accept without qualification any and all reports as to the absolute guilt of the victim. If the various reports conflict, those that indicate the possibility of innocence or of mistake are rejected. Too often the charge of rape is brought in by the spectator mob, even when the original charge will not permit it to be considered.

The mob leaders, actuated by motives best known to themselves, recruit the actual lynch mob from the pool halls and beer parlors, as has been said. The spectator mob is created by the usual methods of the ballyhoo. Publicly to whip up the emotions of the populace is dangerous; there are too many sane persons in any community who would seek every means to prevent the proposed murder. Only the known lynch-minded are informed, and the statement is made in the form of a foregone conclusion: "A nigger will be lynched at Slayden at sundown." "Be at the courthouse at eight. You know why!" Only the lynch-minded respond, and the anti-lynchers avoid the scene. Should anyone opposed to lynching raise his voice, he is warned, boycotted, or labeled "nigger-lover." Wisely he remains at home.

The methods used to produce this audience are the conventional advertising of commerce: newspaper announcements, telegraph, telephone, the radio, word of mouth, and, less commonly, the United States mail. It is direct advertising and its appeal is to the local carnivora. As each lynch-enthusiast gets the news he passes it on, elaborating on the crime the victim committed, whetting the listeners' appetite for blood by suggesting the methods to be employed. Automobile owners make up parties and journey long distances to witness a hanging or a burning. An announced "slow-burning" will bring out the largest crowds.

As early as 1893, Cutler notes, railways were used to augment the spectator mob. On January 31, 1893, Henry Smith, a Negro charged with murder, was publicly burned at Paris, Lamar County, Texas. Excursion trains were run for the occasion and there were many women and children in the throng that watched the sufferings of the victim.

The automobile cut deeply into this neglected feature of railroading, but modern trainmen, schooled in the doctrine of service, may be of help in an informative way. Witness the lady returning to Maryville, Missouri, on a Burlington train, Saturday, January 10, 1931. "Getting home just in time," said the conductor. "They're going to lynch that nigger Monday." Sure enough, Raymond Gunn was burned to death in Maryville on Monday the twelfth.

"Memphis, Tennessee, with its men of mighty beards, of cowhide boots and bowie-knives, was once famous as a boat-landing where captains stopped to hang offending travelers." [1] It is still an important lynch center, strategically located; the lynch-minded of seven states can be summoned within a few hours. If there happen to be hostile officers at the scene of a proposed lynching, there is a conjunction of state lines that can be crossed with little delay or loss of numbers. The Memphis press, through its frequent

[1] Bancroft: *Popular Tribunals.*

92

editions, will keep the lynchers posted and direct spectators over the shortest route to the *ridotto*.

In 1917, Ell Person, a confessed ax-slayer, was wanted by the mob. He was being held in Nashville for safekeeping when the glad news was printed in the newspapers that he would be brought back to Memphis the evening of May 21. Fifteen thousand persons read and answered the summons. Again in 1921 *The Memphis Press* repeated its role of barker and made the burning of Henry Lowry an outstanding lynch success.[2]

When John Hartfield, Negro farm laborer charged with assault on a white woman, was snatched from the law by a lynch gang at Ellisville, Mississippi, in June, 1919, the *Jackson Daily News*, principal newspaper in the state, carried the announcement of the exact time and place in the headlines. Ten thousand persons attended the burning and were addressed by the District Attorney, T. W. Wilson, while the lynching was in progress.

In 1934, the Marianna, Florida, lynching of Claude Neal[3] was ballyhooed over the Dothan, Alabama, radio station, and seven thousand persons from eleven states answered the invitation. In 1935, Ab Young,

[2] See Chapter Six: "Some of Judge Lynch's Cases": The Burning of Henry Lowry.

[3] See Chapter Six: "Some of Judge Lynch's Cases": The Law Never Had a Chance.

Negro accused of murder, was held by the mob until an obliging Memphis newspaper could publish the announcement: "Persons around Mt. Pleasant, Mississippi, are saying that a Negro will be lynched at sundown at Slayden." The Memphis *Press-Scimitar* sent a reporter over the sixty-three miles of road to cover the event, and he arrived forty minutes ahead of the lynching, even though it was held two hours in advance of sundown. The drollery of the County Prosecuting Attorney in this case should not be lost: "So far as the proof is concerned, we don't know whether it was a hanging or a suicide."

After the ballyhoo has brought the event to the point of a great popular uprising, when the spectator mob is en route to the carnival or returning to its homes and firesides, choking the roads and endangering one another's lives, the officers of the law have to be relieved of other duties to direct traffic. While Matt Williams was being barbarously tortured in the public square in Salisbury, Maryland, the police were directing traffic so that the lynching would not be interrupted. Again, when Gunn was to be burned in Maryville, Missouri, the traffic became badly snarled, and it was only due to the snappy work of the Maryville police that the entire mob was able to witness the lynching.

94

In legal jurisprudence the aim has always been to make the punishment fit the crime. An eye for an eye has been the yardstick, and it is only when a crime becomes too prevalent that a heavier or harsher penalty is devised for offenders: the Federal kidnaping act may be cited as an example. In Judge Lynch's court the enormity of the offense has but little relation to the penalty. Here what counts is opportunity, imagination of the mob leaders, the time element. Another factor is experience.

No death seems to be too bad for a Negro; whites are seldom burned, seeming to rate the quicker methods of shooting, hanging, and drowning. If the mob is in complete control of the situation, without fear of gubernatorial or other interference, there are opportunities for protracted orgies that are limited only by the imagination of the lynchers. If there is danger that the National Guardsmen or state troopers may intervene and time is important, it may be necessary to dispose of the victim by the quickest method possible. But mobs also become blasé; a hanging or other quick execution no longer sufficiently satisfies; burning, especially protracted tortures followed by slow burning, are necessary to attract the spectator-mob interest.

Torture is often resorted to to extract a confession

from the victim. Confessions so obtained would not stand up in any other court. In many cases where the prisoner has been taken from jails or courts, after he has either been found guilty or confessed to his crime, the mob will torture him to extract another confession. Raymond Gunn had confessed to the County Attorney, and the confession had been published in whole or in part in the Missouri newspapers, where it was read by all literate mob members. Yet, before Gunn was burned, he was compelled to confess his hideous crime at the scene. The average mob, however, does not need a confession, convinced as it usually is that the victim is guilty, that it has the right man.

Torture used to extort a confession and torture practised as punishment to fit the crime differ not at all. Hanging and lowering just before death, a favorite Mississippi practice, is used in both instances. Gouging of eyes, cutting off of ears and nose are choice bits of mob mayhem, which may be protracted by cutting off the fingers and toes joint by joint. While the victim is still in the hands of the lynchers, members of the spectator mob often invade the sacred circle and use their pocket knives to stab and cut. Corkscrews have been used to tear the flesh from the body and, in 1930, at Ocilla, Georgia, a mob tried to make its victim swallow a sharpened pole. Wire-pliers are used to extract teeth, and gasoline blow-torches, in 1937, were introduced to peel the skin from the bodies of the mob's two victims.

Death often mercifully intercedes during the protracted tortures, but even death does not stop the bestiality. In the case of Claude Neal the mob exhausted its collective energies in torturing its victim, and was at last compelled to put him to death. It managed to summon sufficient energy to fasten the dead body to the rear of a car and drag it to the scene of the original crime, where it was turned over to other mobs for further mutilation and indignities.

Burning with torture has long been reserved as an especial death for Negroes. As early as 1708, it was recorded that a Negro named Sam, accused of murdering the family of his white master, was burned at the stake at Jamaica, now a part of New York City, and put to all possible torments as a terror to others. Water was given him from a horn fastened to a pole to allay his thirst and so prolong the suffering.

Lynching by burning is the vengeance of a savage past and survives today only in the United States. Even the savage did not devise any death so horrible, even to the spectator, as slow burning. Fire is started at the victim's feet and he is literally burned to death by inches, sometimes remaining conscious until the lower limbs are already in ashes. In the larger lynch-

97

carnivals, especially when the victim is a Negro charged with rape upon a white woman, burning is used because it is more spectacular and because through the shrieks and writhings of the victim the spectator mob is brought into a closer relation to the criminal lynch mob.

Part of the ritual of a well-conducted lynching is the unsexing of the victim. George Hughes was unsexed after death in the presence of women and children. The symbolism is simple: the mob-desire to destroy the symbol of creation. In cases of burning, the victim is unsexed before lynching, and in shooting and hanging, after death. In the case of Wesley Everest the unsexing was an act of purest sadism. There is a ritual followed in this perversion, and, at a certain moment, one of the mob leaders steps forward and performs the operation. In certain cases he may be the father or husband of the original victim.

White women who have been lynched were not degraded before or after death. Negro women who attract the attention of lynchers are, regardless of age, invariably mob-raped before being executed.

Chapter Five

THE JURISDICTION OF JUDGE LYNCH

LYNCHING today is as American as apple pie. The practice does not prevail in Canada or in Mexico. Lynching, hand in hand with the Constitution, follows the flag, and follows it across the mountains and the seas. Canada could not stand as a bar against its introduction into Alaska, and neither the Atlantic nor the Pacific Oceans were wide enough or deep enough to stop the Hanging Judge. In Cuba, Puerto Rico, and the Philippines Judge Lynch set up his kangaroo court and brought in his single decision almost from the minute of American occupation. Even peaceful Hawaii has known the violence of Judge Lynch.

Though Judge Lynch today finds most of his cases in the southern states and the great majority of his victims are Negroes, the Judge is ready at all times and in all sections to bring in his grisly verdict. From Aroostook County, in northern Maine, along the Canadian border to the Pacific Coast, down to the Rio Grande, no section of the country is without the blood-stained marks of lynch-executions. Only four

states can boldly proclaim that since 1882 Judge
Lynch has been considered incompetent within their
borders: Massachusetts, Vermont, New Hampshire,
and Rhode Island. If one could only gloss over the
condign summary punishment of working men in all
four states, there might be reason to become lyric over
their records.

One finds it difficult to become lyrical over sunny
California, to stand in admiration of the majestic
mountainous coast of the Northwest or the breeze-
swept vistas of old Florida; too many listless, dangling
shadows, slowly swinging to the winds, mar the pleasure. The shadows cross and re-cross the land and give
little comfort to anyone. That they are decreasing
yearly may be a matter for gratification, but, as the
chart-lines show a decline in numbers, others show a
sharp increase in torture and bestiality.

Five other states are entitled to a but slightly fly-
specked crown for meritorious conduct. Arizona,
Idaho, Maine, Nevada, and Wisconsin have no recorded lynchings of Negroes.

Let's look at the record!

MISSISSIPPI

Mississippi's most important crop is cotton, but her
production of that commodity is surpassed by that of
Texas. In the matter of lynch-executions and the low

degree of bestiality expressed by her mobs, she reigns supreme. Since 1882 this state has conducted more than 11 per cent of all the lynchings in the country, 591 out of an ignoble total of 5,112, and but forty-four of the victims were whites. Only in one recorded year, 1932, has the state been without a single lynching, but its enviable effort in that year did not invalidate its standing. Mississippi leads in the number of women lynched—fourteen, of whom one was a white (1898); in the number lynched whose offenses were unknown; and in the number who could not be identified after death. She shares with Georgia and Texas the records for lynch-executions for no offense whatever. She stands alone in the wide number of fantastic offenses for which her mobs demand the lynch penalty and in originating and putting into effect newer and more barbarous forms of torture.

To this damning indictment may be added the episode at Duck Hill, in 1937.

The Magnolia State has had thirty-three double and nine triple lynchings, again topping all other states. In her records of multiple lynchings she has on six occasions lynched four at a time and has found three opportunities to claim five victims. Her various centers of civilization and culture have enjoyed some excellent lynch-carnivals: Vicksburg, eight; Jackson, five; Yazoo City, six.

Her mobs are responsive and easy to rouse and usually large, though on occasion (1934) as few as four Mississippians can successfully conduct a lynching, especially if the victim is a Negro aged seventy who has merely "talked disrespectfully" to his white landlord. Her mobs are made up of resolute and determined men who are able to outwit the ablest and cleverest sheriffs. In one year two Negroes accused of murder had been sent to separate jails, miles apart, to circumvent any attempt at mob-reprisal. After a year in their respective jails, they were being returned in separate parties for trial. Two mobs, working like teams, were formed and snatched the prisoners from the deputy sheriffs, joined forces, and hanged the accused men to the same tree.

In 1918, four Negroes, all of them minors—Major Clark, 20; Andrew Clark, 15; Maggie Howse, 20, and Alma Howse, 16—were taken by a mob from a jail at Shubuta and lynched from a bridge over the Chickasawha River. They were *suspected* of having murdered Dr. E. L. Johnston, a white dentist.

An investigation conducted by the National Association for the Advancement of Colored People disclosed the fact that Johnston had been having illicit relations with both Maggie and Alma Howse; that Major Clark, who worked on Johnston's plantation, wished to marry Maggie. The dentist had gone to Clark and warned him to leave his woman alone. This had led to a quarrel that was made more bitter when it was learned that Maggie was to have a child by the white man. Later it was revealed that Alma, the younger sister, was also pregnant by Johnston.

Shortly after this episode the dentist was found mysteriously murdered. The finger of mob-suspicion pointed to Major Clark, though there were some who held to the theory that Johnston had been killed by another white man who had accused him of seducing a white woman. The Mississippi mob was not to be cheated by any such theories nor by the fact that both girls were pregnant.

Mississippi mobs prefer the torch and faggot to the rope, and even burning alone does not always satisfy their sadistic lusts. In 1925, Jim Ivy was taken from the officers of the law and burned at the stake for an alleged attack on a farmer's daughter. Ivy had been taken to the hospital for identification by the attacked girl; she was not certain, but he looked like the man who had assaulted her. That was identification enough for the Rocky Ford mob, and Ivy was taken to the scene of the attack and lynched.

Another outstanding characteristic of Mississippi mobs is their determination to get their man; nothing is permitted to stand between them and their quarry. The chase is part of the rare sport. In 1904, Luther

Holbert, Negro, of Doddsville, had a quarrel with James Eastland, a white man, and with another Negro, John Carr. The white planter was killed in the dispute that arose when he came to Carr's cabin, found Holbert there, and ordered him to leave the plantation. Carr and another Negro named Winters were also killed. Holbert and his wife fled the plantation and the man hunt was on; two innocent Negroes were shot and killed before the mob took the Holberts. There was no charge against the woman, but simple facts like that do not deter Mississippi's mobs.

"They were tied to trees, and while the funeral pyres were being prepared they were forced to suffer the most fiendish tortures. The blacks were forced to hold out their hands while one finger at a time was chopped off. The fingers were distributed as souvenirs. The ears of the murderers (sic) were cut off. Holbert was beaten severely, his skull was fractured, and one of his eyes, knocked with a stick, hung by a shred from the socket. . . . The most excruciating form of punishment consisted in the use of a large corkscrew in the hands of some of the mob. This instrument was bored into the flesh of the man and woman, in the arms, legs, and body, and then pulled out, the spirals tearing out big pieces of raw, quivering flesh every time it was withdrawn." [1]

[1] Vicksburg (Mississippi) *Evening Post.*

After the mob had wearied of its sadistic frolic, it is supposed, they mercifully burned the Negroes to death.

It is probably easier to get lynched in Mississippi than in any other state. The ideal American is supposedly the man who works with his hands and thus prospers, takes loving care of his family, building honestly for their future; if he can lend a helping hand to his fellowman in passing, so much more to his and his community's credit. Not so in Mississippi. Take these two cases of March, 1935.

In Lawrence County the body of R. J. Tyronne, a prosperous Negro farmer, was found shot to pieces in the woods near his home on the night of the twenty-sixth, where he had been lynched by a mob of white Mississipians about four days previously. *Tyronne was said to have been too prosperous for his white neighbors.*

Four days later, at Hernando, the body of the Reverend T. A. Allen, of Marks, a Negro, was found weighted down with a chain in the Coldwater River. His only crime had been the effort to organize the sharecroppers of his neighborhood.

Sometimes a Mississippi mob has difficulty in making up its mind as to the best manner of lynching. There are various schools of torture. While a Brookhaven mob in 1928 decided that the Bearden brothers should be hanged, the ritual to be observed caused a schism; one was taken by the adherents of one form and the second by the dissenters. The first brother was tied to the back of an automobile and dragged through the city streets before being carried out of town and hanged; the other brother was hurried off in a car in the opposite direction and hanged from a bridge.

In 1934, at Hernando, De Soto County, where the lynching of Negroes has long been regarded as a public necessity, the lynch-execution of three Negroes was prevented by the startling expedient of calling out the National Guard. Judge Kuykendall apologized for the presence of the troops by saying:

". . . there are now several anti-lynching bills pending in Congress. The effect of these bills would be to destroy one of the South's most cherished possessions—the supremacy of the white race—and I believe a lynching in this case would have effect inevitably in the passage of one of these laws by Congress." [2]

GEORGIA

Georgia is a proud state and Georgians are a proud people. It is a diversified state: Atlanta is known as the capital of the New South, and Savannah shares with Vicksburg, Mississippi, and Charleston, South

[2] Twenty-fifth Annual Report (1934), The National Association for the Advancement of Colored People.

Carolina, the honor of being one of the last stands of the unreconstructed rebels. Georgians the state over point with pride to their state's leadership in many departments of human endeavor and, for all one knows, there may even be a few Georgians who are proud of the state's record of lynch-executions. Although the state has to bow to the superior leadership of Mississippi in the practice of neck-cracking, it can claim that it has lynched fewer white men in proportion to blacks than any state in the Union. In point of numerical lynchings, it led all the other states in the years 1919, 1921, 1930, 1932, 1933, and 1936.

Since 1882 the Buzzard State has lynched no less than 570 persons (November, 1937), of whom only thirty-nine were whites; of the 531 Negroes liquidated, six were women. One was Mary Turner, whose killing brought forth one of the most gruesome expressions of bestiality recorded in modern times. Of the Negroes executed by mobs, two were lynched for no reason at all, ten were killed for offenses unknown and unrecorded, and sixty-one lynch-victims were unknown in the communities in which their bodies were found. Negroes have been lynched in Georgia because they were unpopular, for throwing stones, and for window-peeping. In Salt City, in 1917, two Negroes were lynched for disputing a white man's word.

The Gem of the South has had, since 1882, thirty double and ten triple lynchings. In her record of multiple lynchings Georgia mobs have twice had four victims, and on four occasions they have had five. In December, 1894, a Brooks County mob lynched seven Negroes; in June, 1905, the citizens of Oconee County achieved what they believed to be an all-time high of eight victims, seven of whom were charged with murder and one with rape. In 1918, Brooks County was again drenched with blood, and Georgia's record for mass-lynchings was established with eleven black victims. With this ignominious total she shares second place with Louisiana; Arkansas still holds the unenviable record of having lynched the greatest number at a single *ridotto*.

The scenes of Georgia's lynch-executions are well-distributed over the state; no one locality, save the ill-famed county of Lowndes, can lay claim to distinction for any numerical score, nor can the state centers of culture and commerce dodge the accusation that, at some time within the last fifty years, their citizens have on occasion pushed aside the legally constituted judiciary and summoned the rump court of old Judge Lynch.

Only in Mississippi and Arkansas do mobs equal Georgian barbarity and savagery in lynch-executions. In April, 1899, Samuel Hose, a Negro farm worker, had a quarrel with his employer over wages due. The farmer was killed and Sam Hose escaped. The mob that sought him lacked, in the minds of the leaders, the required ginger, and the man-hunt was pepped up with the added charge that Hose had raped his employer's widow. When he was captured, the Negro confessed to the murder but refused, even under torture, to confess to the second crime.

"In the presence of nearly two thousand people, who sent aloft yells of defiance and shouts of joy, Sam Hose (a Negro who had committed two of the basest acts known to crime) was burned at the stake in a public road. . . . Before the torch was applied to the pyre, the Negro was deprived of his ears, fingers and other portions of his body with surprising fortitude. Before the body was cool, it was cut to pieces, the bones were crushed into small bits and even the tree upon which the wretch met his fate was torn up and disposed of as souvenirs.

"The Negro's heart was cut in several pieces as was also his liver. Those unable to obtain the ghastly relics directly, paid more fortunate possessors extravagant sums for them." [3]

Georgian vengeance is long, and it will go to any lengths to achieve its grisly ends. On more than one occasion Judge Lynch has proved his court to be the

[3] New York *Tribune*, April 24, 1899.

dominant court of that realm, reversing the highest courts and setting aside decisions and sentences that were not in accord with his own limited views. Judge Lynch's court is unlike the legal courts of appeal in that he does not wait until cases are brought to him for a rehearing; in Georgia he has on occasion gone right into the courts of justice and snatched his victims from under the nose of the presiding judge.

In 1904, two Negroes, Paul Reed and Will Cato, were on trial in Statesboro, Bulloch County, for the atrocious murder of the Hodges, a white family. They had already been convicted and were before the bench for sentence when the mob broke into the courtroom and carried them off. In spite of the plea of the brother of the murdered man that the law be allowed to take its course, the two Negroes were burned to death in the presence of a large crowd. That was April 16. The day following was given over to rioting in which many citizens were beaten because their skins were black, and Albert Roger and his son were lynched for no other reason. Miles away, in the same Bulloch County but in the town of Portal, Sebastian McBride, a respectable Negro, was beaten, kicked, and shot to death for trying to defend his wife, who was confined with a three days' old baby, from a whipping at the hands of a white mob.

In 1908, Statesboro again gave way to its tradi-

tional jitters, and on February 17 lynched an unknown Negro on a charge of rape and, a week later,
another Negro, Gilbert Thompson, on the same
charge. Later, far too late for the two Negroes, they
were proved innocent.

Sidney Johnson was a Negro peon whose fine of
thirty dollars had been paid by a white farmer. Smith
had the reputation of ill-treating his Negro employees,
and Johnson rebelled. After having suffered beatings
and abuse, the Negro shot and killed his employer as
he sat in his window at home; he also shot and
wounded Smith's wife.

For this crime a mob of Georgia whites scoured the
surrounding country for more than a week, engaged
in a hunt for the guilty man. Failing to find him, they
began to kill every Negro who could even remotely
be identified with either the victim or his slayer. Will
Head, Will Thompson, Chime Riley, Eugene Rice,
Simon Shuman, Hayes Turner, and three unidenti-
fied Negroes helped expiate Johnson's crime. Mary
Turner, who was within a month of confinement,
loudly proclaimed the innocence of her husband, crying out maledictions on the mob and threatening to
swear out warrants for their arrest. She was herself
taken out and lynched: hanged head downward while
gasoline and motor oil were thrown on her clothing
and set afire. Life still lingered in the dead body, and

a member of the mob stepped forward and with his pocket knife opened the abdomen. The prematurely born child fell to the ground, and the cruel surgeon then crushed its head with his heel. Before the mob dispersed, further pleasure was derived from using the mother's body as a target for pistol practice.

The murderer, Sidney Johnson, was at length discovered in a house in Valdosta. The house was surrounded by a posse headed by the chief of police, and Johnson elected to shoot it out. Before his ammunition was exhausted, the fugitive had wounded the chief. When the house was entered, he was found dead. His body was mutilated.

When the courts of Georgia are not dominated by mobs, as in the Leo Frank case, or overruled by mob law as in the Bulloch County case related above, they sometimes co-operate with the mob. In 1911, Thomas Allen, a Negro, was in jail on a charge of attempted rape and Foster Watts was being held on a charge of "loitering in a suspicious manner." The Judge ordered Allen brought to Monroe for trial and, though the Judge knew that citizens had organized a mob to lynch the prisoner, refused to accept the troops offered him by the Governor. Allen was sent to Monroe in the charge of two officers; the train was stopped and the prisoner hanged beside the tracks. The mob then proceeded to Monroe and snatched Watts from the jail and hanged and shot him. Judge Brand on a previous occasion had refused proffered troops with the statement that he "would not imperil the life of one man to save the lives of a hundred Negroes." [4]

It is not necessary to commit a crime nor to be suspected of one to be lynched in Georgia. As recently as 1933, in the town of Newton, the body of T. J. Thomas, a middle-aged Negro, was found hanging to a tree. No reason for the lynching could be given, no clues to the slayers could be found, and no arrests were made. Three days later, at the same place, was found hanging the body of Richard Marshall, a middle-aged Negro. No reasons for the lynching could be given, no clues to the slayers were found, and no arrests were made.

These incidents may explain the resolution adopted on November 29, 1937, by the Georgia House of Representatives and sent at once to the Senate. It charged that the Anti-Lynching bill, then pending in Congress, was "manifestly unjust, unfair and would work an oppressive burden upon the entire South." No comment.

TEXAS

Recorded lynchings in the Lone Star State are a little confused. The totals do not resolve themselves

[4] *The Crisis*, August, 1911.

into blacks and whites, but also include Indians and Mexicans who may have been either white or Indian. Since 1882 there have been 549 lynchings (1937) involving 384 Negroes, 128 whites, 36 Mexicans, and 1 Indian. Fifty-five of those lynched were unknown by name, twenty-two were lynched for no known reason, and one for no reason whatever. Seven were women, of whom two were white, and one was a case of mistaken identity.

Texas has had twenty-three double and twelve triple lynchings. On three occasions Texas mobs have had four victims, one had five, and four had six. In 1897, a record was set with seven that was not broken until 1908, when eight victims were claimed. Texas mobs achieved their all-time high in 1915 when they lynched near Brownsville ten Mexicans who were charged with train-wrecking and murder. Since the Armistice, Texas mobs have lynched sixty victims; nineteen were shot, twenty-three were hanged, twelve were burned, two were flogged to death, and four came to their deaths by means unknown.

In 1891 a Cass County mob lynched two Negroes for being troublesome; others were lynched for gambling, window-peeping, marrying a white woman, and eloping. The latter case was that of a white minister, a Reverend Captain Jones, of Paris, Lamar

County. Texans are touchy and resent any form of irregularity.

The year, 1922, when Texas romped off with numerical dishonors, she achieved a total of sixteen out of a national total of sixty-one lynchings. May was the banner month in Texas, ten being the total for the month of merriment; of the year's total, eight victims were taken from officers or jails.

In August, 1916, the simple citizens of San Benito got so much pleasure out of lynching six Mexicans on the charge of pillage and murder that they spent the next two weeks assembling six more Mexicans whom they lynched on the charge of banditry. As a matter of record it seems that 1916 was a bad year for Mexicans in Texas; twenty-six of their total were lynched in that year, but many of these cases were the result of border trouble with Mexico.

Texas mobs have little to distinguish them from other mobs. There is a directness about them that is not found elsewhere, and only on occasions do they stoop to the savagery of their sister states. They do err, like others, and at times let Judge Lynch take over their most sacred tribunals of law. In 1895 a Negro was lynched for riding his horse over a little white girl and inflicting serious injuries upon her. Later the mob found that the guilty man had escaped and the

Negro lynched was innocent, but he was already too dead for them to do anything about it.

Dan Davis, a Negro, was burned at the stake at Tyler for the crime of attempted rape, May 25, 1912.

"There was some disappointment in the crowd and criticism of those who had bossed the arrangements, because the fire was so slow in reaching the Negro. It was really only ten minutes after the fire was started that smoking shoe soles and twitching of the Negro's feet indicated that his lower extremities were burning, but the time seemed much longer. The spectators had waited so long to see him tortured that they begrudged the ten minutes before his suffering really began.

"The Negro uttered but few words. When he was led to where he was to be burned, he said quite calmly, 'I wish some of you gentlemen would be Christian enough to cut my throat,' but nobody responded. When the fire started, he screamed, 'Lord, have mercy on my soul,' and that was the last word he spoke, though he was conscious for fully twenty minutes after that. His exhibition of nerve aroused the admiration even of his torturers." [5]

Texas lays claim to one of the largest mobs ever assembled, 15,000. There is, of course, a fine distinction between the mob and the spectators; the mob does

[5] *The Crisis*, June, September, 1912.

the actual work of securing the victim, making all preparations, and finally killing him. In the case of Jesse Washington, the actual mob was 1,500 and the balance, no one of whom attempted to stop the execution, merely accessories before the fact.

Jesse Washington was a defective Negro boy of about nineteen years, unable to read or write; he was employed as a farm hand in Robinson, a small town near Waco. One day the wife of his employer found fault with him, whereupon he struck her on the head with a hammer and killed her. There was some, but not conclusive, evidence that he had raped her. He was arrested, tried, and found guilty, and sentenced to death by hanging within ten days of the commission of the crime.

As the sentence was pronounced, a mob of 1,500 white men, who feared the law's delay, broke into the courtroom and seized the prisoner. He was dragged through the streets, stabbed, mutilated, and finally burned to death in the public square in Waco in the presence of a crowd of 15,000 men, women, and children. The Mayor and the Chief of Police witnessed the lynching.[6]

In 1930, a mob in Sherman, unable to intimidate the officers who were holding the person of George Hughes for trial on charges of assaulting a white

[6] *Thirty Years of Lynching in the United States.*

woman, achieved their desire by burning the court-house in which the Negro was jailed.

In 1935, in Colorado County, a mob of 700 persons, many of them women, took two Negro boys, aged fifteen and sixteen, from the officers who were taking them to face a charge of murder, and hanged them to a tree. The County Attorney, who should have prosecuted the lynchers, said: "I do not call the citizens who executed the Negroes a mob. I consider their action an expression of the will of the people." The County Judge, before whom the lynchers should have been tried, said: "I am strongly opposed to mob violence and favor orderly process of the law. The fact that the Negroes who so brutally murdered Miss Kollman could not be adequately punished by law because of their ages prevents me from condemning those citizens who meted justice to the ravishing murderers last night." [7]

Judge Lynch concurring.

LOUISIANA

Louisiana, with only 421 lynchings to her credit, hardly belongs in the big company dominated by Mississippi, Georgia, and Texas. Her high rating is hardly justified today, for she has had but thirty-six lynchings since the Armistice, and only her previous

[7] *The Crisis*, January, 1936.

numerical strength keeps her so high on the list. Of
Louisiana's total of 421 (1937), sixty-two were white
men, three were colored women, and one was a white
woman. Three were lynched for no offense whatever, eleven for offenses that could not be determined
by investigators, and forty-six victims were unknown
in the communities in which their bodies were found.
There have been twenty-nine double and twelve triple
lynchings since 1882. On three occasions mobs have
had four victims, and on one, five. In 1891 a New
Orleans mob invaded a jail and lynched eleven Italians
who had been convicted of murder. In 1894 a mob
at Talullah, in Madison Parish, lynched seven Negroes
charged with murder.

Such centers of civilization as New Orleans had six
lynchings with seventeen victims; Shreveport, eleven
lynchings, each mob content with a single victim;
Baton Rouge, four. Talullah, with only three lynchings, rolled up a total of twelve victims, but has had
no lynch-executions since 1906.

Louisiana mobs are fallible, like those of other
states. In 1892 a mob was seeking John Hastings, a
Negro of Calaboula, for murder. Failing to find John
at home, they lynched his son and daughter. Three
days later the mob caught up with the murderer and
completed the job. Again, in 1899, at Lindsay, a town
near Jackson, there had been an attempted assault on

a white woman by a Negro, Val Bages. Mitchell Curry, a white farmer, hearing that someone was in his cornfield, took two Negroes with him to drive away the intruder. He proved to be a large Negro, and Curry, becoming convinced that he was Bages, gave chase and finally treed him. The man was ordered to remain in the tree while one of his pursuers went for a rope to hang him, but he slid down and was shot to death. Examination showed that his clothing was that worn at the State Insane Asylum at Jackson, and investigation proved that he was an inmate who had escaped a few days before. Wandering at large, he had suffered death for a crime that he had not committed.

In 1914, at Sylvester Station, three Negroes were lynched for the murder of the postmaster. One, an old man, bore an excellent reputation in the neighborhood; there was no evidence against him and, under duress, he refused to confess to the crime. He was burned at the stake in the presence of a large crowd.

The Houston (Texas) *Post*, commenting editorially on the lynching, said:

"The conviction is irresistible that the old man who was burned to death had nothing whatever to do with the crime. If he had been guilty, the torture to which he was subjected would have forced a confession, and the wonder is that he did not confess any-

how, in the agony of his roasting flesh, as many innocent victims have done in the vain hope of escaping
torture. In all probability the guilty murderers of the
village postmaster are at large, while the blood of in-
nocents rests upon the hands of those who took it
upon themselves to discharge the functions of the
law." [8]

In 1897, William Gordon, of Jefferson, was lynched
for disobeying ferry regulations, and, in 1910, Laura
Porter, Negress of Monroe, was lynched for keeping
a disreputable house.

Lynching offenses in Louisiana include miscegenation, slapping a child, making threats, insulting a lady,
vagrancy, and bringing suit against a white man.

Louisiana can boast one of the few lynchings conducted by Negroes. On August 3, 1934, at Caddo
Parish, Grafton Page, a thirty-four-year old Negro,
was beaten to death by members of his own race because of an alleged insult by Page to a colored girl
who had gone out riding with him.

ALABAMA

Alabama sits pleasantly in the deep center of the
Lynch belt and, through the use of the radio and the
automobile, her mob-minded citizens can participate
in and have participated in lynchings in Georgia,

[8] *Thirty Years of Lynching in the United States.*

Mississippi, Tennessee, and Florida. The Cotton State has an unenviable record of her own: 375 victims, of whom fifty-five were whites and eight were colored women. Forty-one were unknown in the communities where their bodies were found, but only four suffered death for offenses unknown, and two through mistaken identity. Alabama mobs have had fourteen double and twelve triple lynchings. Lynch-carnivals have claimed four victims four times and five victims twice. In 1891 the citizens of Choctaw County got together and lynched seven white men for outlawry, and therewith established the state's record.

Since the Armistice was signed there have been forty-two persons lynched, of whom twenty-six were shot, three hanged, three beaten to death, one cut to pieces, and one burned. Eight came to their deaths by means unknown to the investigators. Lynching scenes are evenly distributed throughout the state, and such important centers as Montgomery and Birmingham have had seven and four lynchings respectively. Alabama mobs seldom descend to the bestiality exhibited by her sister states of the Lynch belt, and only once in recent years has one run hog-wild; when the smoke cleared away there were four dead Negroes and two dead white men.

Clarence Boyd, filling station operator at Geiger,

seven miles from Emelle, picked a bad time to try to collect three dollars and a half that Esau Robinson, Negro, owed him for a second-hand battery. It was July 4, 1930, and a large number of Negroes had gathered at an Emelle Negro church for a picnic. Clarence Boyd happened to be there, and he demanded payment for the battery; when it was refused, he lifted the battery from the Robinson car and placed it in a store at Emelle, refusing to let Esau have it until he had paid for it. Esau left to get the money.

At four that afternoon Esau returned, accompanied by his father, Tom, two brothers, Ollis and King, and a cousin also named Robinson. The Negroes were armed and were drinking. They searched the stores of Emelle until they found Clarence Boyd. Motioning him outside the store, Esau hit him over the head with a bottle. Boyd called to his uncle Grover for help, and as the latter approached, old Tom hit him with a heavy stick. Grover ran to his car for his pistol and began firing at Tom who, though wounded, made his escape. While Boyd was still firing at Tom, either King or Ollis Robinson came up behind him, took aim, and fired. Grover Boyd fell dying, and another member of the Robinson family fired several shots into him. With the exception of Esau, all the Robinsons made their escape. A white merchant held on to Esau and tied him to a post to await the coming of the sheriff.

When the sheriff arrived, he was told that Esau was not the man who had killed Grover Boyd. Leaving the Negro tied to the post, he went in pursuit of the fleeing Robinsons. Some time before midnight Esau was released from the post and shot to death by a mob of less than fifty persons.

The armed man-hunters converged on the home of farmer-preacher John Newton Robinson, brother of Tom and uncle of Esau. John would not give up his gun nor would he permit his house to be searched. In the resulting quarrel he was shot to death and a white overseer, a member of the posse, was killed, probably unintentionally, by a member of the mob. The sheriff, believing that the fugitive Robinsons were hiding in the house, ordered it fired. There were no Robinsons within, and the mob went on with its hunt. On the night of the fifth, Winston Jones, Negro, received a fatal shot at Narkeeta, Mississippi, just across the state line, for failing to stop when ordered. Later in the night a Negro woman, Viola Dial, who was in a car with her husband and three other men, was shot when the driver refused to stop the car at the order of the man-hunters.

For weeks the search for the fugitives went on, but

the mob-minded had deserted and the search was brought to an end by State Enforcement Officers. Tom Robinson and his sons, Ollis and King, were taken to Kilby Prison at Montgomery. Others of the Robinson family, including women and children, were confined in Kilby for safekeeping and as witnesses.

Certain Negroes, familiar with the Emelle community, reported that the altercation over the battery was the immediate but not the real cause of the outbreak. According to them, the trouble grew out of the insistence of certain white men upon "running with" the Robinson and other Negro women.

The persistence of Alabama mobs and their high standing in their communities is best shown by the recent ill-smelling Scottsboro cases. Seven colored boys were sentenced to death on the testimony of two disreputable women, neither of whom knew the meaning of the phrase "sexual intercourse" but only of the usual gutter term. Even when one of the girls recanted her story, only a nationwide clamor could obtain new trials for the defendants.

ARKANSAS

Although Arkansas has achieved the distinction of having been the scene of the largest lynching carnival in the history of the industry, her lynch-executions lack distinction: her mobs merely take their victims out and dispose of them with dispatch. Since 1882 there have been 315 lynchings; sixty-nine of these involved whites, two of them women charged with or suspected of murder, and five colored women. Only one was lynched through mistaken identity, four for offenses unknown; thirty-two were unknown in the communities where their bodies were found.

Arkansas mobs have held eleven double and six triple lynchings. On four occasions they have had four victims and, in 1899, the good folk of Little River lynched seven on the charge of murder. In 1904 the white citizens of St. Charles, Arkansas County, went berserk and destroyed thirteen of their colored fellowmen in an orgy of race prejudice, establishing the state and nation records for known lynch-executions.

Of the state's centers of fashion and culture, Hot Springs leads with a total of six lynchings; Pine Bluff follows with five, Little Rock with four, and Arkansas City with two, one of which was a triple lynching. Since the Armistice there have been thirty-three persons lynched; fourteen of these victims were mercifully shot, thirteen were hanged, three burned, and three went to their deaths by means unknown to the investigators.

If there is one thing an Arkansan dislikes more than a black skin, it is the white skin of a class-conscious sharecropper. So far the record shows that the dominant whites are content with slapping such about, whipping and beating them out of the state. That none have been killed is due only to bad marksmanship; enough shots having been fired.

FLORIDA

In 1903, when Cutler completed his records of lynchings, Florida was placed ninth in numerical order; in Walter White's records (1927) she was placed seventh, a position she still holds. However, in the number of lynchings since the Armistice, Florida is securely in third place. Of the 290 victims of lynch-executions since 1882, only thirty-one were whites; three were women. Florida mobs are willing to destroy for alleged offenses, but none were lynched for no offense or through mistaken identity. Forty-six were unknown to the communities in which their bodies were found, and the offenses of eight were undetermined by investigators.

Florida has had sixteen double and seven triple lynchings. On two occasions the mobs have had four victims and on one, five. In 1911 and 1916 they had six victims, but the state's record was established in

1897, when eight blacks were executed on the charge of murder.

Since the Armistice, sixty-eight Floridians have been lynched, of whom twenty-eight were shot, eighteen hanged, seven burned, four drowned, and one beaten to death. Ten came to their deaths by means unknown.

While the city of Ocala seems to lead the state in number of lynchings, eight with nine victims, Tampa has achieved in fewer years the same number of victims in but six lynch occasions. Lake City also had six lynchings, but with only the same number of victims.

Florida mobs may be distinguished for their directness; they will not be put off when they lust for blood. In August, 1916, in Newberry, a Negro farmer named Boisey Long was accused by white farmers of hog stealing. The sheriff and the white man who had sworn out the warrant for Long's arrest went to take him. Both white men were shot, the sheriff later dying of his wound.

Boisey Long escaped and when the mob came to get him they had to be content with his wife, Stella, and a friend of hers, Mary Dennis. The two Negresses were taken to jail where, it is said, they were tortured to secure information. Two other Negroes, Bert Dennis and Andrew McHenry, were arrested and tortured. The mob, failing to find Long, had shot a Negro named James Dennis, Bert's brother, and when Bert had gone to Newberry to get a coffin they had seized him and thrown him in jail. The mob continued its search and, its blood lust running high, hanged a Negro preacher, Josh Haskins, because he happened to be a neighbor of Long's. Then they went to the jail and secured the four prisoners and took them out and hanged them. Mary Dennis was the mother of two children and was pregnant; Stella Long had four children.

Long was finally apprehended and indicted for the murder of the sheriff and for shooting the man who had sworn out the warrant for his arrest. None of the lynchers was indicted.

The other sextuple lynching occurred in Lake City in 1911. A Negro named Norris and a white man quarreled over some trivial matter, and the white man made a murderous attack on the Negro. The matter was brought before a justice of the peace, and the Negro was exonerated. Later the white man went to the Negro's house, accompanied by some of his friends, and reopened the quarrel. A shooting affray followed, in which one white man was killed and another wounded. Norris and the friends he had with him awaited the coming of the sheriff and surrendered. Six of them were arrested and sent to Lake City for safekeeping. A party of lynchers gained admission to the jail by means of a forged telegram and secured the prisoners under the pretext of taking them to Jacksonville for greater protection. They then took the Negroes to the outskirts of Lake City and shot them to death.

TENNESSEE

Though Tennessee stands eighth in numerical order, she has less than half the number of lynchings of Mississippi to her credit. Of Tennessee's 275 lynch-executions, only fifty-three involved white men and two white women. Three Negresses were lynched; twenty-eight victims were unknown by name, and six were executed for unknown offenses. Only one suffered through mistaken identity.

Tennessee mobs have had twenty-one double lynchings and five triple lynchings. On one occasion the mob had four victims and on another six. Since the Armistice there have been but eighteen persons lynched; of these nine were shot and nine were hanged. Lynchings have been well distributed throughout the state, though a small place named Tiptonville has succeeded in rolling up a lynch-total of twelve victims in seven lynchings. Memphis has had five; Nashville, three; Chattanooga, two; and

Knoxville, one. Ripley, another small town, has managed to stage five lynchings, one a double.

In 1901, at Rome, a Negro named Crutchfield stole a purse. He was taken from the sheriff by a mob and started for the place of execution. In some way he managed to escape, and this so enraged the mob that it took the Negro's sister out and lynched her.

Tennessee mobs continued their ungallant conduct in 1911. Ben Pettigrew, a successful Negro farmer, and his two daughters were on their way to Savannah (Tennessee), taking a load of seedcotton to a cotton gin. On no known provocation they were ambushed by four white men who shot the father, hanged the daughters, and then drove the load of cotton under the tree from which the bodies dangled and set fire to it. *Two of the white men were ultimately hanged for their part in the lynching.*

Tennessee's greatest lynching carnival was held in Memphis in May, 1917. Ell Person, confessed ax-murderer of a 16-year-old white girl, was burned to death in the presence of 15,000 men, women, and little children. The mother of the murdered child cheered the mob as they poured oil on the Negro and set him afire. *The Memphis Press,* in reporting the lynching, said that the mob "fought and screamed and crowded to get a glimpse of him, and the mob

closed in and struggled about the fire as the flames
flared high and the smoke rolled over their heads.
Two of them hacked off his ears as he burned; another tried to cut off a toe, but they stopped him."

Jim McIllherron was a Negro who resented the
slights and insults of white men; he went armed, and
even the sheriff was afraid of him. On February 8,
1918, at Estill Springs, he got into a quarrel with
three young white men. Threats were made, and Mc-
Illherron fired six shots, killing two of the whites. He
then fled to the home of G. W. Lynch, a colored
clergyman, who helped him to escape and was himself shot and killed by the mob. McIllherron was captured and arrangements made for a gala lynching.
Men, women, and children came to Estill Springs
from a radius of fifty miles. The Negro was chained
to a hickory tree while the mob howled about him. A
fire was built a few feet away and the torture began.
Bars of iron were heated, and members of the mob
amused themselves by holding them close to the victim, at first without touching him. One bar he grasped,
and as it was torn away all the inside of his hand came
with it. Then the real torture began, lasting twenty
minutes.[9]

During this time, while his flesh was slowly roasting, the Negro never lost his nerve. He cursed those

[9] *The Crisis*, May, 1918.

who tortured him, and almost to his last breath derided the attempts of the mob to break his spirit.

In 1934, at Shelbyville, Bedford County, a minor lynch center, a mob assembled to take E. K. Harris, who was on trial for criminal assault; they were repulsed by state troops who killed three and wounded twenty more. The mob was so enraged at losing its victim that it burned down the $150,000 courthouse.

KENTUCKY

Since 1882 Kentucky has had 236 lynchings; of these eighty-three involved whites, three of them women, and two, colored women. Twenty of those lynched were unknown in the communities where their bodies were found, and six were executed for no known offense. Kentucky mobs have staged twelve double and three triple lynchings, and on two occasions have had four victims. On November 13, 1914, Night Riders took ten unknown Negroes from the town of Rochester and hanged them for reasons best known to the riders. Of the three white women lynched, one was executed with her husband and two other members of her family for making threats, one on the charge of murder, and the last as a result of mob-indignation. What made the mob indignant is not recorded. The two Negresses were charged with murder.

Most Kentucky lynchings have been confined to the smaller communities. Among the larger cities, Frankfort has had two; Shelbyville, three, with six victims; Paducah, three—one a double lynching; and Bowling Green, two. Since the Armistice there have been ten lynchings; four of these were hangings, three shootings, and three of the killings were by methods unknown.

Kentucky mobs do their jobs thoroughly. At Shelbyville, in January, 1911, a mob felt it its duty to give two Negroes the hemp cure for insulting white women. They took the two young Negroes from the jail and then, as a sort of afterthought, returned and secured an old Negro who was awaiting death sentence. *The Chicago Tribune*, reporting the affair, stated:

"All three Negroes pleaded for their lives but the lynchers paid no attention to them. The lynching was devoid of the minor brutalities that frequently mark such occasions. There was no abuse of the prisoners. The mob was made up of quiet, determined men whose mission was to execute but not to torture."

The rope used on the two younger Negroes broke and they made a dash for liberty, but were riddled with bullets. The mob numbered only twenty men, all masked.

SOUTH CAROLINA

Only nine of South Carolina's 180 lynch victims were whites. Of the 171 Negroes, seven were women, two were executed through mistaken identity, fourteen were unknown in the communities where their bodies were found, and one's offense was unknown. South Carolina mobs have held thirteen double and three triple lynchings; in 1889 they found eight victims and again, in 1898, they found eight more. Aiken, the between-season resort of the *bon ton*, seems to have achieved an unenviable reputation as a lynch-center; three carnivals produced seven victims. Columbia, the capital, has had but one, and Charleston has a clean bill of health. Barnwell and Phoenix share honors in octuple lynchings.

There have been nineteen lynchings since the Armistice; thirteen of the victims were shot, one hanged, two beaten to death, and three died by methods unknown to the records.

The alleged miscarriage of justice is what turns honest South Carolinians into mobs. In 1916, at Abbeville, Anthony Crawford, a wealthy Negro farmer, came into town to sell a load of cotton. He had an unfortunate run-in with a white storekeeper over the price of the cotton, and cursed him. For that he was thrown into jail and released on bail of fifteen dollars. Enraged at this miscarriage of justice, a mob pursued him into a gin mill and became further infuriated when he tried to defend himself. He was dragged out, beaten, kicked, stabbed, and partially blinded before the sheriff rescued him and took him back to jail. Later in the afternoon the mob broke into the jail, dragged the Negro through the streets to the fair grounds, hung him to a tree, and riddled his body with bullets.

Prohibition provided Aiken with its greatest lynching bee. A sheriff and three deputies were sent to arrest Sam Lowman, who was suspected of selling whiskey. Sam was away, but his wife and daughter, Bertha, were at home; when they saw the four white men, wearing no insignia to indicate their official positions, they ran into the house. The officers surrounded the house and the sheriff entered and struck Bertha in the mouth with his fist. The girl's mother started to her defense and was shot through the heart by one of the deputies. A son and nephew, working in a nearby field, heard the screams and shots and hurried to the rescue. In the shooting that ensued, the sheriff was killed and Bertha, her brother, and her cousin seriously wounded.

The trial of the three Negroes was dominated by the Ku Klux Klan, of which the dead sheriff and his deputies were known members. The two Negro boys were sentenced to death and Bertha Lowman was given life imprisonment. The Supreme Court of South Carolina, on the appeal of a Negro lawyer, granted the three a new trial. So well was the new case prepared that the Judge was forced to direct a verdict of not guilty for Demon Lowman, the son. Fearing a further miscarriage of justice, the mob overpowered the jailer and took the three Negroes to a tourist camp on the outskirts of Aiken.

South Carolina mobs like their little jokes. Before 2,000 men and women the prisoners were told they were free to run as fast as their legs would carry them. Off they started, and a volley of bullets brought the two boys down. Bertha Lowman, with many bullets in her body, was making good her escape when another round of fifty shots brought her down for good.

OKLAHOMA

Oklahoma is the first state outside of the real South to get into big company. Since 1882 she has staged 143 lynchings; ninety-five of the victims were white men, two were white women, two Negresses, twelve Indians, and two Mexicans. Thirty-one were unknown in the communities where their bodies were found, and five were lynched for unknown reasons.

The state has staged nine double and two triple lynchings, two in which there were four victims, and one with five; in 1894 a mob hanged seven horse thieves at a single fiesta. Since the Armistice, Oklahoma has had ten lynchings; four victims were hanged, four shot, one was drowned, and the tenth came to his death by means unknown. One white woman was lynched by Indians for an unknown reason, and the other with her husband for an equally unknown reason.

Oklahoma mobs do not require much reason for lynching. In 1911, at Okemah, Laura Nelson, Negress, was accused of murdering a deputy sheriff who had discovered stolen goods in her house. She and her son, a boy of fifteen, were taken from the jail, dragged about six miles to the Canadian River, and hanged from a bridge. The woman was raped by members of the mob before she was hanged.[10]

Further example of Oklahoman gallantry: In 1914, Marie Scott, seventeen-year-old Negress of Wagoner County, was assaulted and raped by white men. She was alone in the house when the men entered, but her screams brought her brother to the rescue. In the fight that ensued, one of the white men was killed. The next day the mob came to lynch her brother, but, finding he had escaped, lynched Marie instead.

[10] *The Crisis*, July, 1911.

138

MISSOURI

With Missouri the lynch record, in order, returns to the South. In the 120 lynch-executions, fifty of the victims were white men, one was a white woman accused of murder, and one a colored woman whose offense was unknown. Missouri mobs have witnessed eight double and three triple lynchings and have had four victims who were unknown in the communities in which their bodies were found; five were lynched for causes unknown. Since the Armistice, Missouri has had eleven lynchings with eight hangings, one shooting, one burning, and one by means unknown.

Two Missouri lynchings are considered of sufficient significance to be treated fully in another chapter.[11]

VIRGINIA

Of Virginia's 109 lynch victims, twenty-four were whites; one of them a woman who was lynched because of her disreputable character. Thirteen victims were unknown in the communities in which their bodies were found, and three were lynched for offenses known only to the lynchers. There have been

[11] "Some of Judge Lynch's Cases": The Five Thousandth; Three Governors Go Into Action.

five double and one triple lynchings, one with four victims, and another with five. Since the Armistice, Virginia has had but five recorded lynch-executions, and three of these were accomplished by shooting and two by hanging.

Negroes have narrow escapes in the Old Dominion. In 1931, William Harper was convicted of criminal assault on a white woman and condemned to death. At a second trial the "assaulted" woman's escort courageously came forward and testified that she had spent the night of the alleged assault with him. The woman was subsequently convicted of perjury.

NORTH CAROLINA

Of all the states in the South, North Carolina has made the noblest effort to eradicate the crime of lynching. Yet she has had 105 recorded lynchings, in which only twenty-one of the victims were whites; twelve victims were unknown in the communities in which their bodies were found and two were lynched for undetermined offenses. One white woman, a girl, was lynched with an Indian doctor in 1897 for an offense that is still unknown. North Carolina mobs have held six double lynchings. Since the Armistice, nine lynch-executions were achieved by shooting, seven by hanging, and two by methods unknown.

MONTANA

Most of Montana's ninety lynchings involved border warfare or frontier justice and included but two Negroes as principals. One case that is still a stench in American nostrils is that of Frank Little, a cripple, who in 1917 was brutally lynched in the city of Butte.[12] In 1920 a white man named E. P. Lampson who was resisting arrest was burned to death in the streets of Billings.

COLORADO

Since 1882 Colorado has lynched seventy persons, of whom sixty-six were white men. The offenses meriting lynching—that is, inflaming the Coloradoan into mob action—are, in the case of white men, murder, bank robbery, and desperadism. Negroes are lynched on the usual charges, real or alleged.

Colorado has had but one lynching since the Armistice, that of two Mexicans taken from the officers of the law and hanged at Pueblo on September 13, 1919.

NEBRASKA

Mob spirit in Nebraska is aroused by murder, cattle-rustling, arson, and wife-beating. In 1889 and

[12] "Some of Judge Lynch's Cases": Those Who Defied the Bosses.

1895 vigilantes rode wild in Keyapaha County and hanged four for rustling. Fifty-five of Nebraska's fifty-nine victims were white, and she has had but one lynching since the Armistice: in 1919 Will Brown, Negro, was burned to death in Omaha for an alleged attack on a white woman.

KANSAS

On fifty-six occasions Kansans have risen in wrath and lynch-executed the same number of their fellow-citizens; nineteen were Negroes, a high percentage for a western state. On four occasions mobs have conducted double lynchings; murder seems to have been the usual cause. Kansas has had three lynchings since the Armistice; two of the victims were hanged, and the third came to his death by means unknown.

WEST VIRGINIA

On the night of December 5, 1894, Lincoln County White Caps took Mrs. T. Arthur, a white woman, from her home and lynched her for reasons known only to themselves. In 1902, a Negro was lynched for conjuring and another through mistaken identity. With these exceptions, murder and rape seem to be the crimes that rouse mob action in West Virginia. Of the state's fifty-six lynchings, twenty-one have involved white men; on five occasions mobs have found two victims, and on one, three. Since the Armistice, five men have been lynched in West Virginia, three by hanging and two by shooting.

In Bluefield, in 1912, Robert Johnson, Negro, was accused of rape. He gave an alibi and proved every statement he made; when he was taken before the girl who had been attacked, she failed to identify him. She had previously described very minutely the clothes her assailant wore. *The Bluefield police took Johnson out and dressed him to fit the description,* and the girl screamed: "That's the man!" A Bluefield mob dragged Johnson out and severely abused him and then hanged him to a telegraph pole. It was later conclusively established that Johnson was innocent.

INDIANA

Fifty-four lynchings: forty-one whites, thirteen Negroes.

Long Klan-ridden, the state of Indiana had still been free of lynch-executions, though beatings and murders were frequent, from 1902 to 1930, when the mob spirit flared with shocking intensity. In that year, at Marion, two Negroes accused of murder were taken from jail and hanged before a mob estimated to number between 10,000 and 15,000. Young girls and women, some with babies in their arms, urged on the lynchers, and one girl, seated atop an automobile, screamed: "Hang-that-Nigger! Hang-that-Nigger!" Unquestionably the finest example of mob-madness outside of the Deep South.

CALIFORNIA

Fifty-three lynchings: forty-seven whites, two Negroes, three Chinese, one Mexican. Two double and one triple lynching; two lynchings of four, and one of five.

Since the Armistice, California has had four lynchings with a total of seven victims, all white. Six came to their deaths by hanging and one was beaten to death. In 1933, a San Jose mob entered the jail and snatched Thurmond and Holmes, confessed kidnap-slayers of Brooke Hart, and hanged them in a public park.

WYOMING

Forty-one lynchings: thirty-seven whites, four Negroes.

Wyoming has had but one lynching since the Armistice. That was on December 19, 1918, when Edward Woodson, a Negro charged with killing a railroad switchman, was lynched at Green River.

NEW MEXICO

Thirty-nine lynchings, three Negroes.

NORTH AND SOUTH DAKOTA

Thirty-six lynchings, one a Negro.

The two Dakotas were linked in lynch-statistics before they were admitted to the Union in 1889, and no attempt has ever been made to separate them. This may be due to the fact that many of the early lynchings were held at undetermined places. Since the Armistice there have been no lynchings in South Dakota and only one in North Dakota. On January 29, 1931, Charles Bannon, white, confessed slayer of six members of the family of A. E. Haven, was taken from jail, carried to a bridge two miles east of Schafer, and hanged.

ILLINOIS

Thirty-two lynchings, nineteen involving Negroes.

Illinois has had only one lynching since the Armistice. In 1924, William Bell, Negro, charged with an attempted assault on two white girls, was killed by a Chicago mob.

ARIZONA

Thirty-one lynchings, all involving white men or Indians.

Arizona has had no lynchings since 1917.

WASHINGTON

Twenty-nine lynchings with only one Negro victim.

Washington has had but one known lynching since the Armistice. This took place in 1919, when a blood-hungry mob of patriots took Wesley Everest from the jail at Centralia, mutilated him, and hanged him three times.[13]

MARYLAND

Twenty-nine lynchings with but two white victims.

Maryland has had but two lynchings, two bad outbreaks of mob-violence since the Armistice. On December 4, 1931, at Salisbury, Matthew William., Negro, was snatched from his hospital cot by a lynching party of three hundred, dragged three blocks to the courthouse square, and hanged to a tree. He is said to have confessed to the murder of his employer, stating that he was paid but fifteen cents an hour for his work in a basket factory. Two years later, at Princess Anne, not fifteen miles from Salisbury, George Armwood, Negro, said to have confessed to waylaying and attacking an eighty-two-year-old white woman,

[13] "Some of Judge Lynch's Cases": Those Who Defied the Bosses.

146

was taken from jail and hanged by a mob of nearly 2,000. His body was dragged through the main thoroughfare for more than half a mile and then tossed on a burning pyre.

Ohio

Twenty-eight lynchings, twelve white victims.

Ohio has had but one lynching since the Armistice. On June 7, 1932, a mob took Luke Murray from the South Point jail, where he was being held for threatening two white men with a knife. On June 11, Murray's battered body was found in the Ohio River. Four white men were arrested but later exonerated by a jury.

Idaho

Twenty-one lynchings, all white victims.

Idaho has had no recorded lynching since 1911.

Oregon

Twenty lynchings, one Negro victim.

Oregon has had no lynchings since 1914.

Iowa

Eighteen lynchings, two Negro victims.

Iowa has had no lynching since 1907.

147

MICHIGAN

Ten lynchings: seven white and three Negro victims.

Michigan boasted a slate clean of lynchings from 1902 until 1935. In that year Silas Coleman, a Negro war veteran, was shot to death in a swamp near Pinckney by members of the Black Legion "for target practice," or "just to see how it feels to kill a nigger." In 1936, members of this hooded secret order of alleged patriots and regulators killed Charles A. Poole, a white WPA worker for allegedly beating his wife (who later denied she had ever been struck by her husband) and hanged Roy Pidcock, white, whose only known offense was that he refused to join the repressive order.

Eight persons were sentenced to life terms for the lynching of Poole and five received similar sentences for the killing of Coleman. As this is being written, Virgil F. Effinger, reputed head of *les cagoulards*, has been arrested and will be tried on charges of criminal syndicalism and bomb possession.

MINNESOTA

Nine lynchings: four white, four Negro and one Indian victim.

Minnesota had no lynchings from 1896 until 1920, when a Duluth mob in June hanged three Negroes.

PENNSYLVANIA

Eight lynchings, involving two whites and six Negroes.

Pennsylvania's last lynching was in 1911; the affair of that year probably shocked Pennsylvanians out of the lynch-madness.

At Coatesville, Zachariah Walker, Negro, had a quarrel with a constable; the officer was killed and Walker badly wounded. A mob took him from the hospital where he was chained to his cot. The bedstead was broken in half and the man, still chained to the lower half, was dragged half a mile through the streets, thrown upon a pile of wood, drenched with oil, and set afire. When Walker, with superhuman strength, burst his bonds and tried to escape, members of the mob drove him back with pitchforks and fence rails and held him until his body was burned to ashes.

All attempts to indict members of the mob failed. After several who were accused were taken before the Grand Jury, they were given an ovation when they were freed.

149

Utah

Eight lynchings, involving six white and two Negro victims.

Utah has had but one lynching since 1900, and that was in 1925, when Robert Marshall, Negro slayer of a police officer, was taken from jail and hanged near Castlegate.

Nevada

Six lynchings, involving four whites, one Indian, and one Chinese.

Nevada has had no lynchings since 1905.

Wisconsin

Six lynchings, all involving white men.

Wisconsin has had no lynchings since 1903.

New York

Three lynchings, involving two white and one Negro victim.

New York's last lynching was in 1916, in Washington County.

Connecticut

One white lynched.

New Jersey

One Negro lynched in 1900 at Hackensack.

MAINE

One white man lynched in 1907 at Bancroft, Aroostook County.

DELAWARE

One Negro lynched in 1903, near Wilmington.

Recapitulation by States

State	Blacks	All Others	Total
Mississippi	547	44	591
Georgia	531	39	570
Texas	384	165	549
Louisiana	358	63	421
Alabama	320	55	375
Arkansas	246	69	315
Florida	259	31	290
Tennessee	220	55	275
Kentucky	153	83	236
South Carolina	171	9	180
Oklahoma	32	111	143
Missouri	69	51	120
Virginia	85	24	109
North Carolina	84	21	105
Montana	2	88	90
Colorado	4	66	70
Nebraska	4	55	59
Kansas	19	37	56
West Virginia	35	21	56
Indiana	13	41	54

State	Blacks	All Others	Total
California	2	51	53
Wyoming	4	37	41
New Mexico	3	36	39
Dakota, North and South	1	35	36
Illinois	19	13	32
Arizona	0	31	31
Washington	1	28	29
Maryland	27	2	29
Ohio	16	12	28
Idaho	0	21	21
Oregon	1	19	20
Iowa	2	16	18
Michigan	3	7	10
Minnesota	4	5	9
Pennsylvania	6	2	8
Utah	2	6	8
Nevada	0	6	6
Wisconsin	0	6	6
New York	1	2	3
Connecticut	0	1	1
New Jersey	1	0	1
Maine	0	1	1
Delaware	1	0	1
New Hampshire	0	0	0
Vermont	0	0	0
Rhode Island	0	0	0
Massachusetts	0	0	0

Chapter Six

SOME OF JUDGE LYNCH'S CASES

(A) *Judge Lynch's* Cause Célèbre—Leo Frank

On Sunday morning, April 27, 1913, the body of a young girl was found in the cellar of a pencil factory in Atlanta, Georgia. It was early identified as that of an employee of the factory, pretty little Mary Phagan. The man who found the body was a Negro, Newt Lee, the night watchman.

A hasty investigation revealed that the crime had been committed by a degenerate and rapist, and that the last man known to have seen Mary Phagan alive was Leo M. Frank, the factory superintendent. Lee and Frank were arrested.

Within twenty-four hours of the commission of the crime the orderly processes of the law ceased to operate and the mob had taken over the case. From the beginning throughout to the end the malignant presence of the mob guided the action, and before its evil power orderly government cringed and ceased to exist.

Accused of a most atrocious murder, this young Jewish superintendent was put on trial the following summer. Newt Lee, the night watchman, was exonerated from any share in the guilt. Outraged by the barbarity of the crime, certain people in Georgia, and particularly in Atlanta, where the crime was committed, and in Marietta, where the murdered girl's family lived, insisted a victim be found to pay the penalty, and they fastened on the young Jew as the one whose death would most surely satisfy their desire for vengeance. The mob, led by Thomas E. Watson and his weekly paper, *The Jeffersonian*, at this point turned the case over to Judge Lynch in actuality.

The flimsiest evidence was admitted as long as it was detrimental to the prisoner. Certain facts not in the nature of conclusive evidence, such as that Frank had phoned the night watchman at seven the evening before the discovery of the body to learn if everything was all right, were seized upon as proof of guilt.

Whether or not the testimony at the trial was convincing is entirely immaterial in considering the real significance of this case. What made it a noted one was the spirit that pervaded the courtroom and the vicinity of the courthouse—the malevolence of the mob.

The courtroom was thronged with a hostile crowd

of people. The jury had to pass through this crowd on its way to and from the jury box. Outside the courthouse the state militia was deployed for action. The local newspapers had lashed the people of the vicinity into a lynch-frenzy. The crowd in the courtroom was demonstrative in approval of the accusers and the evidence against Frank. He was a Jew. He did not know his place; as superintendent he had had true-blue Americans *under* him. Mary Phagan had been an employee; for the employed class this was convincing proof that the young girl had been helpless.

Inside the courtroom and outside the courthouse the mob spirit was vocal and demonstrative; it yelled for blood and it meant, as the end proved, to have blood. The trial consumed thirty days and the case was turned over to the jury. Can anyone believe that those jurors were insensitive to the mob spirit that was manifesting itself on all sides?

When the jury was ready to give its decision, the Trial Judge and the Counsel did not dare to have the prisoner brought into court; because of the mob spirit, his right to be present and face his accusers when the verdict was given was denied him. If that jury had decided that the evidence they had heard and considered was insufficient to convict, if their verdict had been "not guilty," there was obvious danger to themselves; if their verdict was against Frank, there was equally obvious danger to the prisoner.

The Judge who had presided at the trial in his answer to a petition for a new trial later gave sufficient reason for doubting the verdict of the mob spirit in this case:

"It has given me more concern than any other case I was ever in, and I want to say right here that, although I heard the evidence and arguments during those thirty days, I do not know this morning whether Leo Frank is innocent or guilty."

Frank's absence from the courtroom at the time of his sentence was one of the grounds upon which he appealed his case to the state Supreme Court and then to the United States Supreme Court. The state Supreme Court held that the question should have been raised at a certain stage in the proceedings; since it was not raised then, it could not be raised at all. The highest court in the land said it was a question of procedure that is to be determined solely by the state courts. The mob spirit that dictated the verdict and the absence of Frank from the courtroom was never considered.

During the whole process of appealing the decision, the mob kept up its threats. When the case came before the Prison Commission of Georgia, where the mob's action and influence could be weighed, the mob itself made its voice heard and menaced those who had power to recommend commutation of sentence.

The case was finally brought before the Governor. Governor Slaton was braver than the mob and he dared to ignore its demands. After reviewing the case and taking into consideration the refusal of the Prison Commission to recommend commutation of sentence, he commuted Leo Frank's sentence from death to life imprisonment. It was a courageous action; a lone man against the mob. Governor Slaton had a legal and moral right to do this, and his action did not interfere with the prerogatives of the jury or with the authority of the Prison Commission. He defied the mob and the mob snapped and snarled at his heels. Against the Governor it was impotent, for he himself saw that during the rest of his term it was held in check. Within a few days he left office.

Frank was sent to the State Prison at Milledgeville to finish out his natural life. The spirit of the mob invaded the prison, and soon after Frank entered, his throat was slashed by a fellow-prisoner sentenced for murder who thought the Jew too vile to live.

The mob was not yet done with Leo Frank. On August 17, 1915, while he was still recovering from the attack of his fellow-prisoner, a mob of twenty-five, evidently agents selected by the greater mob, whose power had been growing all these months, entered the prison and, with suspicious ease, overawed the warden and the guards, dragged Frank from his bed in the dormitory, carried him in an automobile to within a few miles of the birthplace of Mary Phagan, and hanged him to a tree. Former Governor Slaton was compelled to flee his native state because of threats on his own life.

The lynching was done with fatal deliberation; it was the result of no hasty, impulsive passion but of cool plottings for weeks in homes and barrooms by hundreds of willing murderers. How, one may ask, were the twenty-five selected from the greater mob? By vote? Or because they knew the interior of the State Prison through previous incarceration? Or was this an occasion when the actual mob leaders took matters into their own hands?

The lynchers believed they had done a solemn duty; in trampling upon the law they believed they had executed justice. Listen to the Marietta *Journal* the day after the lynching in its own town:

"The people demanded that the verdict of the court be carried out, and saw to it that it was. We insist that they were, and are, law-abiding citizens of Georgia."

And race-prejudice got into full flight in Thomas Watson's weekly:

"A Vigilance Committee redeems Georgia and carries out the sentence of the law on the Jew who raped and murdered the little Gentile girl, Mary Phagan. . . . Let Jew libertines take notice."

The mob went even further and let it be known throughout Cobb County and the entire state of Georgia that it would not be safe to try to discover and punish them, for they were determined men.

The fullest accounts of the lynching appeared in all Georgia papers. Every newspaper reader read the story of Frank's death ride; each reader, by referring to his newspaper, could learn all that had happened and all that had been said between Frank and the lynching party on their way from the prison to the place of hanging; how Frank sat in the automobile and how he acted during the trip. The stories recorded every word that had been said to him and every word he replied during the seven-hour journey. The lynch mob, the stories went on, had not been rough with him, and Frank had shown stoicism.

Yet the very day this story broke, the Coroner's jury brought in the verdict that Frank "had come to his death at the hands of persons unknown." Many witnesses had been summoned, but they all declared they knew nothing, had seen nothing, and recognized no one. Only one witness ventured to admit that he had seen two men step out of an automobile near the scene of the lynching and that he had had a pretty strong suspicion of what was going on. This slight admission evidently made an uncomfortable sensation in the courtroom. The Acting Solicitor turned to the witness and very slowly asked:

"You did not recognize anybody?"

The witness moved nervously in his chair and replied:

"Nobody, sir."

At this word there was audible relaxation in all parts of the courtroom.

The man who wrote the revealing story of the lynching, who was either a member of the mob or had had his story, not from a single member of the mob but from several members, was not called. The one witness who could have been made to testify or be declared in contempt of court was not called. It was the final stigma on the formerly fair name of Georgia, the mob's *beau geste* to law and justice and honor.

The leading newspapers of Georgia, as well as those of the rest of the South, condemned the murder of Leo Frank and the expression of mob-law it had evoked. The general tenor of these writers was that it would take the state from twenty-five to one hundred years to live down the disgrace; that Georgia had probably learned its lesson and would, in the future, refrain from recourse to mob-law and lynch-executions.

Since Frank was hanged, Georgia has had 133 lynchings, only two of which involved whites.

(B) *The Mob Was Orderly*—New Orleans Mafia

Lynching was pretty much an affair entirely our own until the beginning of the nineties, when a group of Italians was lynched in New Orleans. Since then the entire world has watched our homely practice with misgivings. Are we an entirely civilized people? Missionaries in Africa complain that our continued lynching of Negroes seriously interferes with their efforts to convert the heathen. Enemies within and without make worth-while capital of our uncontrollable impulse to resolve ourselves into mobs and hoist our fellowmen into the foliage of trees.

In the late eighties and at the beginning of the nineties the Sicilian society known as The Mafia held the Italian population of many large American cities in its power. It was the beginning of racketeering in the United States, and, so long as the extortioners worked among their own inarticulate people, little could be done to stamp out the practice. The victims were warned that if they talked it would be bad for them and their families. The petty extortion involved even the lowliest laborer, who turned over a portion of his wages to his padrone; the richest and juiciest plums came from those Italians who had been successful in business. Here the shakedown ran into the thousands, and no one knew how extensive the gross takings were. Blackmail followed petty extortion and led to kidnaping and even murder. The conditions existed in New York, Chicago, and other large cities with sizable Italian groups. It was in New Orleans, however, that this secret society first exceeded itself.

In 1890 the four-year-old son of a wealthy Italian merchant was kidnaped and held for $75,000 ransom. When kidnaped, the child was healthy and robust; a month later, when he was returned to his parents, his health was so impaired that he died within a short time. The case aroused public feeling to such a point that the police were compelled to take cognizance of the society's criminal activities. Chief of Police David C. Hennessey himself took entire charge of the investigation. Detectives were sent to Italy to trace the records of known members of the order; others were sent to Chicago, St. Louis, and San Francisco, and, within a short time, the Chief knew enough to begin making arrests and to be assured that he would secure convictions.

Late one foggy night, just before the trap was to be sprung, Chief of Police Hennessey was on his way home. As he neared his residence, a boy darted out of the fog, shrilled a peculiar whistle, the Mafia signal, and a volley of bullets mowed the policeman down. He was shot three times in his abdomen, his right knee and left hand were shot through, and his face and neck were horribly mutilated by gunshot wounds. He languished until the next morning, but only one word passed his lips: it was the whispered "Dagoes."

The evidence the Chief had secured was used to round up the members of the society. One, Pietro Monasterio, who lived in a shack within sight of the Chief's home, was arrested. In his house were found six shotguns, five with sawed-off barrels and with stocks hinged so that they might be doubled and carried under the clothing. The boy who whistled the signal and twelve others were arrested; fourteen in all were brought to trial.

The State's case was exceptionally strong and was presented by District Attorney Lionel Adams, who was considered by bar and laity to be an outstanding and able prosecutor. Judge Romon, the presiding justice, was uncompromising, dignified, unapproachable, and a capable judge. Aside from convincing circumstantial evidence, there were eyewitnesses, one young couple identifying no less than eight of the prisoners. The defense was based on the old reliable alibi, backed up with terrorized witnesses.

In Louisiana the jury is competent to fix the terms of punishment in criminal cases and, when this jury brought in their written verdict, the Court was stunned. Twelve of the defendants were sentenced to jail for terms varying from ten to four years and two were declared innocent. Judge Romon looked at the written verdict with horror and stupefaction.

"Bribery," was the first cry, while others claimed the jury had been intimidated. Public indignation flared to such a degree that the convicted prisoners and the two who were acquitted were remanded to the Parish Prison. The verdict had been rendered on Friday, March 13. That evening the New Orleans *Item* and the *States*, and the following morning the *Picayune* and the *Times*, carried the following advertisement:

MASS MEETING

All good citizens are invited to attend a mass meeting on Saturday, March 14th, at 10 o'clock A. M. at Clay's Statue, to take steps to remedy the failure of justice in the Hennessey Case. Come prepared for action.

About Clay's statue the streets were blocked, but the people were orderly and attentive. They were addressed by many leaders, temperately at first. John M. Parker, who later was to become Governor of the state and in 1916 the Progressive party's candidate for

Vice-President, was one of the earlier speakers. Later on the mob leaders took over; one, who remains unnamed, announced rhetorically:

"When the law is powerless, the rights delegated by the people are relegated back to the people, and they are justified in doing what the law has failed to do."

The speaker went on to charge the jury with corruption and intimidation and asked if the people were ready to follow him. The response of the mob was loud and unanimous. Jumping from the platform, he shouldered his way toward the Parish Prison, some two miles distant. Members of the Washington Artillery and the Crescent Rifles fell in behind him, and the demonstration took on the appearance of a well-organized parade, not of a mob out of hand.

The prison occupied a whole square, its main gates giving on Orleans Street. Inside, the wardens and guards heard the constantly growing crowd, and this, with their knowledge of the protest meeting at Clay's statue, warned them what they could expect. Carpenters were called and were jeered while they hastily barricaded the side entrances. The Mafia signal, the shrill whistle, was now used as an expression of derision and was on everybody's lips. Then, to those within the prison, guards and prisoners, came the sound of the tread of footsteps, the cheers of the onlookers as the mob hove into sight. Three patrol wagons of City Police that had been summoned by the warden were disarmed by members of the militia, and the police were placed under military guard.

A nearby lumber yard provided the battering-rams, and the work of demolishing the entrances was soon finished. The mob leaders admitted not more than sixty to the prison and posted armed men at all exits with instructions to shoot any prisoner who attempted to escape.

Ten of the Italians had been confined in a large new steel cell. The mob found it impossible to open the lock, the warden having refused to give up the keys, and their battering-rams failed to gain them admittance. It was decided to shoot the prisoners.

A few minutes were given them for prayer, and then the firing squad went into action. The new steel cell became a shambles, one of the prisoners who had been a leader of the society receiving sixty-eight wounds. The boy who gave the signal on the approach of the police chief was spared, as was Machecia, the second who was acquitted by the jury. The other two prisoners were lynched outside the prison. Monasterio was hanged to a cottonwood tree in front of the prison and his body riddled with bullets. Poloviso, insane from fright, was hanged from a lamppost, but he was too tall and his toes touched the ground. A youngster shinned up the post and, placing a knee on each shoulder, jolted him to death.

The mob then divided into groups with the intention of visiting punishment on the jurors who had taken part in the trials. No jurymen were found; they had all fled the city.

Unlike so many of our lynch-executions, the affair at New Orleans did not end with the demise of the victims; three of the lynched Italians were proved to be loyal subjects of King Humbert. The Italian Consul at New Orleans made his protestations, agreeing that some of the victims were very bad men indeed, but objecting that many of the charges against them were unsubstantiated, baseless, that his request for the military had been ignored, and that he and his secretary had been insulted and all but mobbed. The Kingdom of Italy, too, raised her voice; through the Premier, Marquis de Rudin, relayed through Baron Fava, the Italian Ambassador to Washington, a demand was made for heavy indemnity for the families of the lynched and the immediate extirpation of the lynchers. Mr. Blaine, the Secretary of State, properly expressed his horror and regretted the incident, but pointed out that his Government did not regard indemnity as a right the Italian Government could demand. Summary punishment of the lynchers, the Secretary was able to maintain, would be un-American and unreasonable, since the utmost that could be done would be to institute judicial proceedings, and this function belonged exclusively to the State of Louisiana.

There were threats by the Italians of breaking off diplomatic relations; Mr. Blaine replied that the Italian Government was trying to hurry him in a manner contrary to diplomatic usage and that he would announce no decision until the case was thoroughly investigated. It was, to him, a matter of indifference what persons in Italy thought of our institutions. "I cannot change them, still less violate them."

The Italian Government finally accepted $24,330 to be distributed among the families of the victims, offered "out of humane consideration, without reference to the question of liability therefor."

(C) *The Burning of Henry Lowry*

If the Emancipation Proclamation meant anything to the Negro as a people, it had no place in the life of Henry Lowry. As recently as 1920 this Negro was as much a slave as if he had been sold on the block in the eighteen thirties. But Henry Lowry's master, a white landowner named O. T. Craig, of Nodena, Arkansas, had a better deal than he could have had one hundred years ago. At that time a black of Lowry's heft and ability would have cost him at least $1,500.

In 1918 Craig got his Negro for nothing, made him feed himself, take care of himself and his wife and little daughter in sickness and idleness. The nice name for it is peonage.

For two years Henry Lowry had worked for O. T. Craig without pay. Came Christmas Day, when all the world was gay and merry, but to Lowry it was just another day, and the meal at best would be side meat and potatoes. He thought of the two years of labor without pay; he probably thought, too, that the season might loosen the purse strings of his master. Humbly, as befitted a man of his color and station, he went to his master with his hat in hand and asked for his due. Instead he received curses and blows.

Henry Lowry fought back. The landlord and his son ganged up on him, and the son shot him. Then the black drew his own gun and shot and killed his oppressor; he also shot and killed the landlord's daughter, who had moved in to protect her father. Two sons of O. T. Craig also were wounded, and Henry Lowry took to the woods.

For two days he lay hiding in the cornfield of his friend, J. T. Williams, who fed him while another friend, Morris Jenkins, raised the money for train fare to Mexico. The fugitive managed to get to El Paso, on the Mexican border, but, lacking the money necessary to get across, he was compelled to change

his name and seek work in the border city. The job
he got paid him forty dollars a month, and he wrote
to Jenkins to go to see his wife, who was staying with
a third friend, and give her the message that within
a few months he would be able to send for her and
their little daughter. That was the worst mistake
Lowry made.

The white landlords for miles around Nodena had
been thoroughly aroused by this rebellion of one of
their peons. If Lowry was permitted to get away with
his private revolt, other peons and sharecroppers
would rebel. Class consciously they formed themselves into an avenging mob, dedicating their entire
efforts to tracking down this helot and wreaking
vengeance on him for assailing their feudal rights. So
complete was their espionage that they managed to
intercept the letter Lowry wrote to his friend, even
though it was signed S. M. Thompson.

El Paso was too far away, too expensive a trip for
the mob. The information as to Lowry's whereabouts,
his alias, even the address in the border city where
he was living, were given to the police while the mob
bided its time. Two deputies, Dixon and Greer, were
sent to bring Lowry back to face Arkansas justice.
The deputies had instructions, orders, if you please,
from Governor McRae not to take the fugitive back
to the scene of his crime nor to the county jail. They

were to bring Henry Lowry by the shortest route to Little Rock for safekeeping.

The deputies, it now seems, had a greater loyalty to the mob than to their state and their oath. Instead of following Governor McRae's instructions, they took the fugitive direct to the mob. They brought him by way of New Orleans and were taking him into Memphis, which is many miles away from Little Rock, in a state that had no relation to the crime, and could not possibly be considered on the route to Little Rock. The mob knew the route the deputies would take with their prisoner and stopped the train at Sardis, Mississippi, *overpowering and disarming* the *surprised* officers of the law.

The actual snatching was done by a handful of men early in the morning of January 26, a month after Lowry's attack on his white master. The balance of the mob awaited their fellows at the Hotel Peabody in Memphis; nearly one hundred of them were gathered in the hotel lobby, laughing, talking, and preparing to return to Arkansas come evening. This was to be no mere hanging: Henry Lowry was not to be taken to the nearest tree by an enraged citizenry and strung up. Hanging was too good for this Negro.

The mob dined happily at the Peabody; it was a gala occasion.

In Little Rock Governor McRae was desperately

seeking a method of stopping the lynching. He said:
"I can't get in touch with Sheriff Blackwood, so I
wouldn't know who to send the troops to. *I understand that Sheriff Blackwood is at the Peabody Hotel
in Memphis* and I have tried to telephone him there,
but they say he isn't in his room." [1]

The noon edition of *The Memphis Press* announced
in a headline the full width of its front page:

LYNCHING PARTY ON WAY TO
ARK. TO PASS THRU MEMPHIS

Negro Who Killed Two on
Christmas Day Taken From
Officers at Sardis, Mississippi

"We are going to parade him through Main Street
when we pass through Memphis," the leader of the
mob boasted at Sardis. "Then we are going to take
him to Arkansas and that will be the end of him."

The *Press* insisted upon being helpful to anyone
interested enough to wish to attend the lynching. Its
directions were explicit.

"The mob, it is said, is taking Lowry back to Wilson, Ark., near where he shot and killed two white
persons on Dec. 25, and is to cross the Harahan
bridge over the Mississippi here. . . . As the roads

[1] Reported in *The Memphis Press*, January 26, 1921. Italics are
mine. F. S.

to the Helena ferry are impassable, there is no other route by which they can cross the river."

The home edition of the same paper got into the full spirit of the ballyhoo and promised, in front page headlines:

MAY LYNCH 3 TO 6 NEGROES
THIS EVENING

LOWRY NEARS TREE ON WHICH
IT IS PLANNED TO HANG HIM;
TAKEN THRU MEMPHIS TODAY

RUMORED OTHERS WILL DIE

A professional press agent could not have done better. "Reports received here," the home edition continued hopefully, "indicate that Lowry and three or four other negroes—perhaps even more—are to be lynched at Nodena tonight. The other negroes are alleged to have aided Lowry to escape. . . ."

Were the Memphis police planning to stop the lynching? After the noon edition had announced the route of the lynch mob, the home edition reported: "Police immediately guarded all the roads entering the city [Memphis] to prevent them from bringing the prisoner here. The mob must have learned of this en route from Sardis, for as they neared Memphis Lowry was turned over to five men in a closed car, who skirted the city." In another column the *Press* gave the latest directions. "It is rumored here that the mob will skirt Memphis and cross the Mississippi River in launches at Richardson's Landing, Tenn., just opposite Nodena."

Only the Memphis police tried to stop the lynching. Governor McRae could have called out the Arkansas National Guard, patrolled the river bank, and prevented the landing of the lynching party, but he could not have saved Henry Lowry. The mob was ready to lynch him in any one of three states. But the Governor of Arkansas made no effort to save the other Negroes, either by reinforcing the guards at the penal institutions in which they were incarcerated or by moving them to what is known in the South as "a lynch-proof jail." No obstructions were placed in the way of the mob and its designs save the feeble efforts of the Memphis police.

The Memphis *News Scimitar* was more explicit. In its sixth (final city) edition, it was definitely announced that the mob would cross at Richardson's Landing, where they would be joined by a party waiting on the Arkansas side, "prepared to lynch Lowry promptly at six o'clock." The *News Scimitar's* dispatch was from Millington, Tennessee, and refers to the mob as "a party of seven in two automobiles with Henry Lowry, negro murderer." Later, in the same news story:

". . . . The party stopped at Fowler's restaurant for lunch. The negro was taken into the restaurant and kept under observation while the party ate.

"The negro said nothing, but showed the strain he was under. He realized he was on his way to death. A number of Millington citizens were attracted to the restaurant, and a few accompanied the party to the landing. They are not expected to cross the river.

"Nothing occurred to mar the serenity of the journey. The party ate leisurely and after finishing went to E. A. Harrold's store, where a quantity of rope was purchased. It was said that the rope would be used in place of chains for the automobiles. The road is very bad and slippery at the approach to the landing."

The Memphis Press had done a good ballyhoo job and sent Ralph Roddy, its ace reporter, to cover the lynching; he did it admirably, even if a bit incoherently. He knew his sheet and its audience and he fed both the pap they most desired. To get the picture of the lynching of Henry Lowry as a whole, it is necessary to jump about a bit through Roddy's story.

"More than 500 persons," he wrote, "stood by and looked on while the negro slowly burned to a crisp. A few women were scattered among the crowd of Arkansas planters who directed the gruesome work of avenging the death of O. T. Craig and his daughter, Mrs. C. O. Williamson.

"Not once did the slayer beg for mercy despite the fact that he suffered one of the most horrible deaths imaginable. With the negro chained to a log, members of the mob placed a small pile of leaves around his feet. Gasoline was then poured on the leaves, and the carrying out of the death sentence was under way.

"Inch by inch the negro was fairly cooked to death. Every few minutes fresh leaves were tossed on the funeral pyre until the blaze had passed the waist. . . . Even after the flesh had dropped away from his legs and the flames were leaping toward his face, Lowry retained consciousness. Not once did he whimper or beg for mercy. Once or twice he attempted to pick up the hot ashes in his hands and thrust them in his mouth in order to hasten death. . . . Each time the ashes were kicked out of his reach by a member of the mob. . . . As the flames were eating away his abdomen, a member of the mob stepped forward and saturated the body with gasoline. It was then only a few minutes until the negro had been reduced to ashes."

When Roddy had got all he could from the burning, he anticipated the mob and hurried on to Wilson and Blytheville, where the other Negroes scheduled by his paper to be lynched were incarcerated. He told of his trip and the people he met, but he was compelled to admit in blackface type:

"The almost impassable dirt roads perhaps saved all these negroes from death. The mob was too tired to try to get over them."

If Governor McRae had been unable to locate Sheriff Dwight H. Blackwood in his room at the Hotel Peabody in Memphis, the *Press* experienced no difficulty and was able to secure the following statement from that officer:

"Nearly every man, woman and child in our county wanted the negro lynched. When public sentiment is that way, there isn't much chance left for the officers. Of course, we may believe that the Negro ought to be killed, but as officers it is our duty to carry out the law.

"I knew several days ago that they had men at Texarkana, Hoxie and Jonesboro, and that we wouldn't have a chance of going that way, so we took the only route left open. We found later that they had men at New Orleans and were tipped off when my men left that place. I believe that there were some Arkansas men in the crowd but they didn't let my men see them."

In all the lynching records Henry Lowry is carried as having been burned for the murder of two whites, never for the killing of two fellow humans in what, in this America of ours, must always be called self-defense. But Lowry's skin was black, and for years to come the shadow will darken the state of Arkansas.

(D) *The Law Never Had a Chance*—Claude Neal

Marianna is a city in Jackson County, in the north-western part of Florida, on the Alabama border. It is a shabby, down-at-the-heels sort of place and inhabited by shabby people. It is a tourist stopover, and only travelers in the shabbier cars stop even for a night. It has an imposing hotel and some stores, and a few of the tradesmen have built new homes for their families. Saturday is Marianna's big day, when the rural folk come to trade and do their week's shopping, and for that day there is a degree of activity that has its attractiveness. The balance of the week it is, at best, a very dull town.

Marianna itself has been the scene of several lynchings, and Jackson County has many others, two of them double lynchings, to its credit. All the lynched have been Negroes. Wages are low in Marianna, and morals do not achieve an altogether high in Jackson County. White men openly run with colored women, and white women, not openly at all, are known to have colored lovers. The Negroes of Jackson County know this and deplore the practice, and when it is mentioned shake their heads and shuffle out of ear-shot. The whites deny it and, should the investigator pursue the matter, he is answered with vituperation and threatened with physical violence. It is a lynch country.

It was that way with Lola Cannidy and Claude Neal. Lola was a white girl and Claude a Negro. "For some months," says the white investigator for the National Association for the Advancement of Colored People, "and possibly for a period of years, Claude Neal and Lola Cannidy had been having intimate relations with each other. The nature of their relationship was common knowledge in the Negro community."

Neal's friends had advised him of the danger of the relationship and had urged him to discontinue it.

On the afternoon of October 18, 1934, Lola disappeared from her home. It is alleged that she told her parents, Mr. and Mrs. George Cannidy, that she was going to water the pigs and to attend to some other chores that were part of her tasks about the farm. The family took no particular notice of her absence when she failed to return in the late afternoon. Her brother, who had been working in a nearby field, reported that he had seen her talking to someone. When she still failed to return that night, a search was begun for her in the vicinity of her home. Early the next morning her body, fully clothed, was found by an uncle, John King, a short distance from her home, badly mutilated about the head and arms and partially covered with brushwood and pine logs. A watch, a ring, a piece of clothing, and a hammer were among the articles discovered near the place where she came to her death.

Several boys testified that they had seen Claude Neal near the scene of the crime that afternoon, and that he had some wounds on his hands that he said he had received while repairing a fence. The first home visited by the sheriff was that of Annie Smith, mother of Claude, just across the road from the Cannidy home. The officers claimed to have found some bloody garments in the house.

A search for Claude Neal was started and he was arrested on a nearby peanut farm. He confessed and implicated another man, Herbert Smith. Smith was arrested and with Neal was taken, as is the custom in the lynch country, to a nearby woods and questioned. It was understood that Neal had had a fight with Smith and Herbert had beaten him. Neal finally admitted that Smith had nothing to do with the crime and that he alone was involved. Smith was subsequently released by the officers.

What Neal told the officers in the woods was not revealed. Later he told a friend that Miss Cannidy had informed him that she wanted to break off their affair, that she did not want him to speak to her again, that if he did so she would tell the whites in the community on him. Neal is reported to have said:

"When she said she didn't want me to speak to her and then told me that she'd tell the white men on me, I just got mad and killed her."

With Neal were arrested his mother, Annie Smith, and his aunt, Sallie Smith. Sheriff W. F. Chambliss, sensing the awakening lynch-spirit, wisely ordered that the prisoners be taken to the jail at Chipley for safekeeping.

Lola Cannidy was murdered Thursday, Neal was arrested Friday, and the big day in Marianna's week became the second biggest day in the city's history and the beginning of a week of shameless mob ferocity. The county men drove their women to Marianna as usual and the women did their shopping as usual. The men resolved themselves into little groups in which the common topic was how to "get the nigger." From that moment a bloodthirsty mob relentlessly pursued Claude Neal. And it must be credited to the Jackson County sheriff that he made every effort within his power to circumvent the mobs. The angry mob at Chipley caused the sheriff to remove Neal to Panama City and the two women to Fort Barrancas at Pensacola. Later Neal was removed by boat to Pensacola, and when a mob threatened that jail, he was moved across the line into Brewton, Alabama, two hundred and ten miles from Marianna.

On October 23 the Marianna *Daily Times Courier* said:

"In a determined effort to locate the three Negroes held for the murder of Lola Cannidy near Greenwood last Thursday, a relentless mob continued to search the jails of West Florida."

George Cannidy, father of the slain girl, stated to a representative of the same paper:

"The bunch have promised me that they will give me first chance at him when they bring him back and I'm ready. We'll put those two logs on him and ease him off by degrees. . . . When I get my hands on that nigger, there isn't any telling what I'll do."

On the morning of October 26, a mob of a hundred armed men stormed the Escambia County jail, at Brewton, Alabama, and snatched Claude Neal after jailer Mike Shanholster had unlocked his cell. "We'll tear your jail up and let all the prisoners out, if you don't turn him over to us," the mob leaders had threatened. They also told Shanholster that they were going to turn Neal "over to the girl's father and let him do what he wants with him." The mob came in thirty cars all bearing Florida plates, and the prisoner was placed in the first car for the return trip. No attempt was made by officers to follow the mob.

Within an hour of the snatching, the people of Marianna, more than 200 miles away, knew that Claude Neal was in the hands of the mob, and newspapers all over the country were able to print advance announcements of the forthcoming lynching. Word was passed all over northern Florida and southern Alabama that there was to be a "lynching party to which all the white people are invited." Others got their jubilee invitation through the Dothan, Alabama, radio station, which scored another "first" for the radio. The lynching was to take place in front of the Cannidy home.

How many people responded to the invitation is not known. Marianna has a population of about 3,500 and Jackson County has 30,000 all told. But there were cars from eleven states, and the Chipola Hotel and the rooming houses had a hard time finding room for all the guests. To say that 10,000 attended Marianna's lynch-carnival would be stating it conservatively.

While the mob still held the murderer, it was encouraged by word from the law. Deputy Sheriff S. Paul Greene, of Jackson County, stated, "In my opinion the mob will not be bothered, either before

or after the lynching." Editorially the *Jackson County
Floridian* feebly said:

"Although many have strongly favored the court
of Judge Lynch for the brutal slaying of a Jackson
County girl this week, local officers have spared no
effort to uphold their oath of office and to protect their
prisoner. In many instances this action has been contrary to the wishes of citizens, but the consensus of
opinion is that one crime in a week is enough."

The lynch mob, the original group of a hundred
that had snatched Neal from the Brewton jail, felt
that the secondary or sight-seeing mob was too large
for safety, and that it would be better if they attended
to the lynching themselves. From the time they had
brought him back to Jackson County they had been
submitting their victim to various sadistic indignities
and finally took him to the woods about four miles
from Greenwood.

From time to time during the torture a rope would
be tied around Neal's neck and he was pulled up over
a limb and held there until he almost choked to death;
then he would be let down and the torture would begin all over again. After several hours of this unspeak-
able torture, "they decided just to kill him."

After death the body was tied to a rope from the
rear of an automobile and dragged over the highway

to the Cannidy house. Here the sight-seeing mob, estimated at between 7,000 and 10,000, took over. The rope was cut adrift from the car. A woman came out of the Cannidy house and drove a butcher knife into the dead man's heart. Then the crowd passed in review; some kicked the body and others drove their cars over it. Little children, neighbors of the Cannidys, waited with sharpened sticks for the return of the body and, when it was rolled into the road that night, these children drove their weapons deep into the dead flesh.

The sight-seeing mob felt cheated; it had been promised participation in the actual lynching and all it got was the sight of the already lynched body. The explanation given them by one of the lynchers was that they were fearful that someone would be injured in the melee if they brought the prisoner to the waiting crowd. A Cannidy kinsman stated, "the nigger was too low for anyone to be hurt on his account." The secondary mob, to be appeased, burned the home of Neal's mother, Annie Smith, to the ground.

The horribly mutilated body was next taken to Marianna, a distance of ten or twelve miles, and at three o'clock in the morning it was hanged to a tree in the courthouse square. Scores of citizens viewed the body, which was nude until early morning, when someone had the decency to hang a burlap sack over the middle of the body. It was not cut down until about eight-thirty Saturday morning.

As soon as the body was cut down, the members of the mob quickly dispersed. There were not so many Negroes in Marianna that Saturday. The entire week had been one of terror, and all Negroes who could stayed away from the city. Those who were compelled to remain kept to themselves.

Before noon, a white man and a Negro had a scuffle, and the sight of a Negro resisting a white man threw the crowd of loungers into a fury. The black finally tore himself away and took refuge in the courthouse, where he was given protection by a friendly group of white men. The mob clamored for their victim, but were held at bay by a machine gun. The frustrated mob began a systematic attempt to drive all Negroes from the town. It attacked men, women, and children, and several blind persons were ruthlessly beaten. The Negroes started from the town in droves, some running, some crying, all frightened. After emptying the streets, stores, and places of business of Negroes, the mob started for the residential district to drive out the colored maids. One man, whose wife shielded her maid from the mob, said, "Saturday was a day of terror and madness, never to be forgotten by anyone."

The mob also drove the policemen of Marianna from their posts, and during the rioting the town was without police protection. Members of the mob threatened to beat up any member of the force they found. The Mayor tried to deputize some special officers, but was unable to find anyone who would serve. Then the Mayor called the Governor in Tallahassee. In response to his request, a detachment of guardsmen was ordered from Apalachicola, but a rainstorm saved Marianna. At eleven a downpour so dampened the spirits of the mob that it probably prevented further rioting and terrorism. The guardsmen arrived at four-thirty and quickly dispersed the remnants of the mob.

(E) *The Five Thousandth*—Raymond Gunn

A Texas mob, incited by a woman in a red dress, burned down a courthouse to lynch its victim, and a Missouri mob, led by a man in a red lumberjacket, used a school to make a funeral pyre for Raymond Gunn, who became Judge Lynch's five thousandth recorded victim. Red is a color that irks bulls; it seems to be an appropriate color for the garb of mob leaders.

Raymond Gunn was guilty and he made no effort to conceal it. His crime, that of murder, was committed in a county that had never before had a lynching, had never been laid open to contempt by a mob

187

in any form; a county where the courts functioned rapidly and peace officers were, supposedly, above reproach and loyal to their oaths. Yet, in 1931, the people of Nodaway County, city of Maryville, threw off their veneer of civilization and for a time became savages of the lowest order. They put aside their perfectly good court and filed their case in Judge Lynch's Court of Uncommon Pleas.

Raymond Gunn was known as a bad nigger. In 1925 he had been convicted of attempted rape and sentenced to four years in the state penitentiary. In the prison he was rated as a "smart nigger" and he was released in January, 1928. After returning to Maryville, Gunn made two further attempts at assault on college girls who refused to push the cases because of the notoriety that would result. Shortly after, Gunn married a mulatto girl and moved with her to Omaha.

In 1930, the Negro returned without his wife; she had died supposedly of pneumonia—but, according to many, from the frequent beatings administered by her husband. Some opinions are that Gunn had a criminal record in Omaha, but it seemed hardly worth while to check on that after the Negro had been lynched.

On December 16, 1930, a nineteen-year-old white teacher in the little one-room school at Garett, located about three miles from Maryville, was found brutally murdered. Raymond Gunn was immediately suspected and warrants for his arrest were sent to all nearby peace officers. In two days he was arrested; he still had on the bloody clothes worn when he committed the crime, and his shoe-print fitted the impression found in the soft earth outside the schoolhouse. He was given the third degree, but did not confess until "they tried religion on him." This brought out a complete confession that was heard, in part, by newspapermen from St. Joseph, Kansas City, and other points.

Gunn's confession told of how he had been in the neighborhood of the school on Monday afternoon, passing that day to look at some of his traps, when the idea occurred to him to rape the school teacher. Accordingly, the following day he returned to the schoolhouse to carry out his plan. He lay in hiding until the pupils had gone home and then crept to the window and watched while the teacher made preparations to close the school. She took the coal bucket and went to the coal box outside and filled it. Just as she was re-entering Gunn appeared at the door. She was frightened and he followed her inside. He carried a hedge club in his hand.

In the struggle the teacher bit the Negro's thumb and he swung his club and struck her over the head. She seized the coal bucket and attempted to strike

189

him with it, whereupon he hit her again and knocked
her down. She fell between the desks and he dragged
her out into the aisle.

Here he was interrupted by a passer-by, a girl on
a bay horse riding down the lane in front of the schoolhouse. He watched until she had passed out of sight
and then returned to the teacher. She had revived, and
asked him to give her a drink of water; instead, he hit
her another blow with his club. The examining physician later stated that it was this blow that fractured
her skull and caused her death. Gunn, at this point,
heard another noise and, again becoming frightened,
left without performing the intended rape. The examining physician again reported that the Negro's
statement in regard to this was true; there had been no
rape. Later the prosecuting attorney, after checking
on Gunn's various statements, stated that the confession was complete.

Lynch-feeling was high in Maryville, and Gunn was
removed at once to St. Joseph for safekeeping. All
the next day, Friday, crowds milled around Maryville
talking lynching. Plans were laid to go to St. Joe and
storm the jail, provided it was not too strong and the
officers did not put up too much opposition. When
the mob arrived on Saturday, it found the officers
ready. A unit of the Missouri National Guard was on
duty with a machine-gun truck barring entrance to

the jail; others were mounted on the roof and distributed about the yard. The mob was defeated in its purpose, but it set up a great howl, booing, catcalling, and demanding the person of the Negro. The machine-gun crew on the roof were oiling their weapon; one of the crew swung the barrel back and forth in a way that suggested he was getting the range of the mob. It forgot its booing, evaporated, returned to Nodaway County and Maryville, and that night the prisoner was taken to Kansas City.

Raymond Gunn's trial was set for Monday, January 12. This date was determined by the officials of the court and the Prosecuting Attorney. As soon as the announcement was made, the mob unofficially announced that Monday the twelfth would be the day Gunn was lynched. The mob was right. Gunn never went on trial, at least not in Maryville, Nodaway County, Missouri. Rather, say he was sentenced in that center of culture and civilization and executed at a little higher than usual cost to the taxpayers.

The date set for the trial was given full publicity in all newspapers in that section of the Ozark state. Preparations for the lynching went forward just as surely as preparations for the trial progressed in the Prosecuting Attorney's office. The lynching was deliberately planned; it was known to all Nodaway County that the Negro was not to be brought to trial and it cannot, by any stretch of the imagination, be termed a quick flare-up of mob frenzy. These Missourians of Nodaway County were as deliberate in this affair as they would be in a horse trade or betting on a horse race. The leaders were known, they were Maryville and Nodaway County men; they met in the heart of Maryville and openly discussed their plans.

The Negro was to be seized at the courthouse. Even if the Sheriff and his deputies tried to protect their prisoner, which was not expected, one of the conspirators was to pick him off with a rifle. The point on which these men commonly agreed was that Raymond Gunn was not to come to trial. In so far as they were concerned, he had already been tried, found guilty, and sentenced by the Hanging Judge.

The spectator mob began forming on the Saturday before the trial. Men who came to Maryville for their weekly shopping on this day planned to stay and "see the fun." Those neighbors who lived in distant parts and who did not have first-hand knowledge of the coming lynching were informed of developments by telephone. All day Sunday they received calls, the gist of the message being: "Be at the courthouse at eight. You know why!" By Sunday evening every parking-space in Maryville was crowded with out-of-town

192

SOME OF JUDGE LYNCH'S CASES

cars and the men sat inside them bundled in great
coats and sheepskins, for it was very cold.

The Mayor of Maryville was not ignorant to what
was going on, and he appealed for reinforcements for
the local peace officers. The Governor sent the State
Adjutant General to assist the local authorities in any
way they might need. The Missouri National Guard
may be called out to assist in preserving peace and order
only "at the written request of the sheriff or other
local authorities." This order the Sheriff steadfastly
refused to give, insisting that there was not going to
be any trouble. In view of the common knowledge of
the proposed lynching, the Sheriff's refusal to give
the Adjutant General a signed order can have but one
meaning. The Adjutant General, in the presence of
the Sheriff, ordered the Captain of the local guard
unit to mobilize his men and have them in uniform and
armed by seven-thirty Monday morning. In considering the non-use of the militia, one unanswered question
is why, in the face of the Sheriff's refusal to request
their use in writing, the Mayor did not give the Adjutant General the required document.

The guard unit was ready at the appointed time.
Rifles, side arms, and tear bombs were issued, and the
men put through their drill inside the armory. The
mob, too, was ready, and the leaders posted men at

each door of the courthouse to give warning when the prisoner was brought in. In the light of later events, that was hardly necessary. The court opened at nine and the clerk called the first arraignment, "State versus Gunn," and the Court ordered the Sheriff to bring in the prisoner. While the Judge and Prosecutor waited, the Sheriff left the court, went through the crowds to the jail to secure the Negro. There he found a car with two deputies awaiting him. Gunn was placed in the back seat with one; the Sheriff climbed into the front with the other.

The reporter for the St. Joseph *News-Press* wrote:

"It was an amazing sight; here was the prisoner being taken straight to the mob waiting for him. I was standing there with the editor of the local paper. We ran toward the car, and the crowd nearly beat us to it. 'Here he is!' they yelled, and crowded around the car as it came to a stop just opposite the courthouse entrance on that side. 'Grab him!' several men yelled. I saw the sheriff open his door, and a big man put an arm around him and pulled him over. Another leader opened the back door in the meantime and held the deputy, while a third reached in and seized the Negro. A dozen men swarmed around the prisoner and pulled him out into the street. The sheriff picked himself up, dusted off his coat and walked back toward the jail.

I don't know what happened to the deputies. They just sort of melted away."

The National Guard unit was still in the armory awaiting the call that did not come. The mob, as though by common assent, did not lead their prisoner past the armory but took him through another street. Here the arrangements went awry; there had been no plans beyond the snatching of the Negro. At this point the unknown man in the red mackinaw took command. He mounted the running board of an automobile and announced that they would take the Negro to the scene of his crime and burn him in the schoolhouse. The mob yelled its approval. They would march, continued the man in the red coat, and they would avoid the armory. Miles down the road to the schoolhouse marched the mob with their prisoner in chains.

When they arrived at the schoolhouse, Raymond Gunn's face had been badly mutilated; his nose and ears had been cut and torn. There were still no signs of any resistance on the part of the authorities, although, from the time that the man in the red coat had announced from the running board of the car what the mob intended doing with their victim, the march had consumed no less than one and a half hours. Time for the Sheriff to have gone into action, if he had had any intentions of doing so; time, too, for the

Mayor, who was one of the "other local authorities" mentioned in the state law, to see that the Guard was sent to protect the Government's prisoner. The mob showed far more intelligence than did the city officials.

The simple announcement that the prisoner was to be burned was sufficient for some members of the mob. Disregarding the red-coated man's instructions to march, many drove at once to the proposed scene of the lynching. When the main body of the mob arrived, it found that much of the work of clearing the schoolhouse had been done.

Gunn was taken into the schoolhouse and made to repeat his confession. When he had finished, he asked: "Now what are you going to do with me?"

"Well, nigger," said the leader. "We're going to burn you."

Two members of the mob found a short ladder and mounted to the roof of the schoolhouse. They tore away some of the shingles on either side of the peak, baring the ridge pole. The Negro was pulled up, made to lie prone along the ridge pole, and then was chained to it. Gasoline was sent up and poured over the victim's body and about the top of the roof. Below, car tanks were drained and the gasoline thrown inside the schoolhouse. Then the leader ordered the crowd to fall back while he lighted a paper and tossed it through a window. The interior of the schoolhouse was aflame at once, and in another moment the roof burst into flames about the victim. There was a single long scream from Gunn, then his clothing burned off and the gasoline flames died down. The fire continued and the roof caved in within a quarter hour. Just two and one half hours after he was snatched, Raymond Gunn was dead; they were two and one half hours of sadism that Maryville, Nodaway County, and the State of Missouri will be a long time living down.

Here was a lynching that could have been prevented at any one of a dozen points. One single, determined public official—the Mayor, the Prosecuting Attorney, the Sheriff, the Chief of the police, any one of the Selectmen or members of the city council, the County Clerk—could have summoned the National Guard to to protect the prisoner. Even the Adjutant General could have disobeyed the law and saved the state's honor. The only statement ever made in defense of these public servants came from the supine Sheriff, who said he was unwilling to turn the guardsmen "loose in that crowd with their automatic pistols; somebody would be killed or badly injured, and probably it would have been the guardsmen."

(F) *Twice Lynched in Texas*—George Hughes

Negroes in the South should have learned long before 1930 that they must not ask their white employers for money due them, no matter how long overdue or how badly they may need it. It meant burning to death for Henry Lowry in Arkansas and it brought death in the same form to George Hughes at Sherman, Texas. The law officers of Grayson County tried their best to give the accused Negro a fair trial, but the mob, instigated by an illiterate bootlegger and incited by a woman of questionable reputation, carried the day and incidentally destroyed the county courthouse and a considerable portion of the Negro-owned property.

George Hughes, a forty-one-year-old illiterate itinerant farm-worker, on Saturday, May 3, 1930, went to his employer to collect the six dollars wages due him. His employer, a white renter, was not at home; his wife informed the worker where her husband could be found and said that he would not return from Sherman until evening. The Negro went away but came back less than an hour later armed with a double-barreled shotgun and again demanded his wages. Again put off, he pushed the woman into a bedroom and assaulted her. She begged him to let her go and promised him all the money in the house. Fearing that her small son might give an alarm, he tied her to a bed and told her that he was not through with her and would return. The renter's wife managed to break her bonds and fled across a field to a neighbor's house. At once the neighbors went to res-

cue the child, and they found Hughes walking aim-
lessly about the barn. At the approach of the white
men, he fled.

A deputy sheriff arrested Hughes in a creek bot-
tom, and later announced that Hughes had fired at
him with the shotgun. The Negro confessed his
crime, agreed to plead guilty, and was taken to a jail
some miles distant for safekeeping. His trial was set
for May 9, less than a week from the commission of
his crime.

Within two days highly colored rumors about the
crime were widespread; not only had the Negro
raped the woman, but he had a venereal disease, her
throat and breasts were mutilated, she was not expected to live. Medical examination of the woman
and the Negro proved that all the reports except that
of the rape were untrue. They had served their odious
purpose and Sherman, by the time the Negro was
ready for trial, was sufficiently mob-minded to demand the services of Judge Lynch.

The law officers of Grayson County sensed the
growing mob spirit and sought a change of venue,
but the relatives of the assaulted woman demanded
that the trial be held in Sherman. Hughes was brought
into court on schedule, escorted by four members of
the Texas Rangers. Outside, a constantly growing
crowd made their opinions vocal as the jury was be-

ing selected. People from outside Sherman were constantly arriving and, it was later learned, had been urged to attend the trial by an illiterate horse trader and bootlegger. Cries of "Let's get the nigger right now" were heard, and a woman, dressed in red and unknown in Sherman, circulated among the men, chiding them for their yellowness. A small segment of the mob got into the courthouse and tore an American flag from a corridor wall and paraded about the building; later this group was ejected from the courthouse by the use of tear bombs thrown by the Rangers.

The whipping up of the mob was comparatively ineffective until one o'clock. At this time the woman who had been attacked was brought from the hospital to the courthouse in an ambulance. As she was being taken into the courtroom on a stretcher, the mob became active, vicious, and uncontrollable. Again it charged into the courtroom, and this time was dispersed with a single charge of buckshot and more tear gas. The leader of the Rangers instructed his men not to shoot, and this order was heard by members of the mob. Later it was interpreted as an order from the Governor and one that applied not only to the Rangers and peace officers but also to the National Guard, who were summoned later.

The woman in red continued to rib the young men for their lack of courage and, to prove that they were full-grown men with hair on their chests, they threw stones through the courthouse windows. At this demonstration, the trial judge decided on a change of venue and the prisoner was hurried into the fireproof vault in the district clerk's office on the second floor. A pail of water was placed beside him.

About two-thirty, a young man threw a can of gasoline through one of the broken windows and another pitched in a lighted match. When the gasoline did not ignite, a third lad climbed to the window-sill and struck another match. These boys were recognized as students and former students of the Sherman public schools. The fire department used their ladders to take people from the second floor of the courthouse, and the crowd protested only when it was the turn of the Judge, Prosecuting Attorney, Sheriffs, and Rangers to use the ladders as a means of escape. Finally all were removed save the Negro in the fireproof vault. As the firemen sought to control the fire, the members of the mob cut their hose.

Every attempt made by the firemen and police to save the courthouse was rebuffed by the mob. "Let her burn down; the taxpayers will put her back." By late afternoon the courthouse was gutted and the mob had grown to include practically all the population of Sherman and of the nearby city of Denison. At nightfall some doubts were expressed as to whether or not the Negro was really in the vault, and arrangements were made to blast it open.

Earlier in the evening the Rangers had telephoned Governor Moody for reinforcements, and a small detachment of National Guardsmen arrived at this time. The mob greeted the soldiers with hoots and catcalls and later with bottles and bricks from the burning building. One woman, a mother, held her baby aloft, over the heads of those in front of her, and screamed:

"Shoot it, you yellow, nigger-lovin' soldiers!"

The militiamen, realizing they were outnumbered, retreated to the county jail, some three blocks away. At seven, another detachment of more than fifty arrived from Dallas and were posted as guards about the already totally destroyed courthouse.

The mob still gave credence to the "don't shoot" rumor and they wanted the Negro, dead or alive. After dark, a pitched battle between the troops and the mob took place, and the troops were thrown back to their headquarters in the county jail. Several soldiers were badly cut and beaten and many had their rifles taken away from them. The mob, again in complete possession of the scene, sang "Happy Days Are Here Again" as a victory song.

By eight o'clock the embers of the courthouse had cooled sufficiently to permit attempts to open the second-story vault. The structure resisted all methods until an acetylene torch was applied. A hole was made and a charge of dynamite inserted and detonated. One of the mob leaders entered, and the body of George Hughes was thrown to the waiting wolves. Whether the Negro was baked to death or killed by the dynamite blast is not known; part of his head was blown off and the water bucket that had been placed in the vault with him was empty.

The corpse was dragged behind a Ford containing two young men and two girls to the Negro section, a distance of less than half a mile. The entire mob followed, yelling, still singing "Happy Days Are Here Again," tooting automobile horns: a gala night in the old Lone Star State. These people were not through with George Hughes. In the center of the Negro business district, in front of the Smith Hotel, they paused and hanged his body to a cottonwood tree. A further touch of sexual perversion was added to the necrophilism of the night when a mob leader unsexed the body in the presence of men, women, and children. The Smith Hotel, Negro property, was denuded of chairs, tables, and other furniture to build the pyre under the hanging body. While the body was roasting, the mob took everything of value from the hotel; chewing gum, confectionery, soft drinks were passed about the crowd, and then the hotel was fired. The mob resumed its singing and dancing about the fires. When the hotel fire died down, the crowd went to the Andrews building, a two-story structure owned by Negroes, and fired that, deserting the old fire for the new. They, the members of the mob, openly boasted that they would burn the home of every Negro in town, and they proceeded with their self-appointed task.

One house was occupied by a white tenant, though owned by a Negro. The mob considerately helped the tenant move out his personal goods and then set fire to the house. Negro property owners called upon the police, the fire department, the Rangers, and the National Guard for protection, but the police were too busy directing traffic, and the entire attention of the fire department was being given to saving white-owned property. One white man, named Sofey, whose son was later indicted as a member of the actual mob, saved a row of Negro-owned residences by falsely swearing to the mob that he was the real owner.

At four o'clock in the morning enough troops were sent to Sherman to put the mob to rout. Before they arrived, the destruction, in addition to the courthouse, included a hotel, the Odd Fellows Hall, the Knights of Pythias Building, a life-insurance office, theater, two cafes, two undertaking establishments, two dentists' offices, two doctors' offices, two barber shops, a drugstore and many residences.

Meanwhile, all of Sherman's two thousand-odd Negro citizens were under cover; some were given refuge by white friends and employers. The others with babies and the aged and the sick hurried away in whatever conveyance they possessed or upon foot. Some found refuge with Negro friends in the country and adjacent towns, but many spent the night hidden in ditches and ravines and under bushes.

Dawn found the city of Sherman quiet and under martial law. There were threats heard to engage the troops in combat and to continue the job of driving the Negroes out of town. Dawn, too, found notices posted on the homes of Negroes, warning them to leave town or suffer the consequences. One white employer was notified, by the poster method, to discharge his Negro workers and replace them with whites. The Negro citizens who returned, under the protection of the troops, were persecuted and abused before the situation became normal again.

On the following Monday, May 12, a military court of investigation was set up for the purpose of securing evidence for the Grand Jury. Of sixty-six

men and women questioned by this court, twenty-
nine were arrested and jailed to await whatever action the Grand Jury should take. Three women were
arrested, but no indictments were drawn against them.
The two young men and two girls whose Ford had
dragged the body were not identified and the family
of the victim of the assault was exonerated of all responsibility for the lynching and rioting.

Of the fourteen indicted, only one owned any tax-
able property, and a new courthouse is costing the
county $100,000. And there are other items to be
added to the bill: rent for offices for county officials;
expenses for guardsmen, Rangers, and other state officers sent to the scene; and the salaries of the fifty
men who served under the Director of Public Safety
when martial law was lifted. Ironically enough, the
Negroes who suffered most, losing their life savings
in fire and smoke, cannot collect on insurance policies
because of the riot clause. When Hughes' burned
torso was cut down, it was offered to the town's two
Negro undertakers, but since both had been burned
out of business, it was turned over to a white under-
taker.

On the night of May 9, 1930, Black Friday as it is
now known, the city of Sherman gave strength to the
statement made years ago by old Bill Sherman. He
said: "If I owned Hell and Texas, I'd rent out Texas."

(G) *Three Governors Go Into Action—1933*

The almost constant decrease in the number of lynchings since the high of eighty-one in 1919 to a low of eight in 1937 received a severe setback in the first year of President Roosevelt's administration. Nineteen-thirty-three had twenty-eight known lynchings, and during the last four days of November, American newspapers carried lynch-news almost to the total submergence of other matter. During those days the Governors of three widely separated states, yet each with its capital approximately on the line of the thirty-ninth parallel, went into action in varying manners and with decidedly varying results. In two of the states Negroes had been lynched; in the third, two white men had lost the decision before Judge Lynch.

On October 18, a Negro, George Armwood, was taken from the jail at Princess Anne, Maryland, and hanged by a mob of 2,000. After the lynching, the body was dragged through the main thoroughfare of the town and burned in the public square. Governor Albert M. Ritchie demanded the arrest and conviction of the leaders. After a month of inaction from the authorities of Somerset County, he gave the names of nine alleged lynchers to the Maryland National

Guard and sent a provisional battalion of 300 men to make the arrests. The Governor did not declare martial law; a provision of the Maryland Constitution gives him power to use the National Guard to quell riots or enforce the law.

To make the arrests the troops were compelled to act with military precision and to employ war-time strategy. They moved secretly from Baltimore in a fleet of eleven buses, followed by trucks carrying field kitchens. At Salisbury they took over the town's armory and waited while a detail of State Troopers raced along the deserted roads at two in the morning, taking over the Princess Anne telephone exchange and stopping all calls to prevent word of the arrival of the troops from spreading over the wires. Then they went to the homes of the nine men for whom they had warrants, routed from bed those they could find, four all told, bundled them into a truck, and sped back to Salisbury.

Here the prisoners were taken to the armory and turned over to the waiting guardsmen. Two of the warrants were invalid, one having been made out for a fictitious name and another in the man's nickname. Of the other alleged leaders for whom warrants had been issued, one was in Virginia and two had escaped. The bed of one of them was still warm when the troopers came for him.

In the face of extremely bitter criticism from Eastern Shore people, Governor Ritchie defended his action:

"The State Government cannot stand by and permit a State's Attorney to decline to arrest persons who are reliably charged with crime, and, as long as neither he nor the judges would act, it became my duty to put in motion the machinery of the law and cause the arrests to be made."

The crowd around the armory in which the four prisoners were held increased as the news spread. Three thousand heard that the guardsmen were going to take their prisoners back to court at Princess Anne for a hearing.

"Like hell they will," one man gave voice to the mob's thought. "They're not taking them anywhere." This defy was greeted with cheers, and the mob became menacing. The National Guard officers told off a hundred men to fix their bayonets, issued them tear bombs, and posted them about the building. This show of strength further infuriated the mob and there was danger that the press from the rear would force those in front into the bristling steel. Suddenly the Adjutant General ordered: "Let them have it!" The soldiers threw their bombs into the mob, blinding some to tears and leaving others gasping. The bombs had a demoralizing effect for a few minutes, and the mob retreated, only to re-form and again advance threateningly. A second tear gas barrage was more effective, and the mob pressed back out of the zone of danger.

Later in the morning the mob, reinforced by more farmers and more oystermen, again attempted to break through the line of troops outside the armory, but were again repulsed with tear gas; this time it was used in such quantity that from then on the mob stayed behind what might be called the menacing point. The Guard officers and the State Troopers had a conference, and it was decided that it would be unwise to attempt to take the prisoners to Princess Anne, a dozen miles away. The temper of the mob was such that anywhere along the route they might expect pitched battles or sniping from roadside bushes. The four prisoners were hustled into buses and, almost before the mob was aware of it, they were on their way to Baltimore for, as the phrase goes, safekeeping.

The mob, cheated, looked about and saw those it considered responsible for its predicament: newspaper correspondents, photographers, and newspaper trucks. The reporters were forced to flee to cellars; the photographers, recognizable by their cameras, were easy prey; later, when the delivery trucks were bringing papers, they were met, their loads destroyed, and their drivers forced to return to their home towns.

The following day the Governor's prisoners were returned to Princess Anne on habeas corpus proceedings and taken before the very judge who had refused to issue warrants for their arrest and *freed for lack of evidence and witnesses*. Governor Ritchie sharply rebuked the judges sitting in the case, charging that they knew that "evidence entirely sufficient" to warrant holding the accused men "would be promptly produced if they were willing to hear it."

Judge Lynch was not reversed. Governor Ritchie and the Free State of Maryland did everything in their power to punish the guilty; there is no stain on the honor of either. But the people of the Eastern Shore, and particularly of Somerset County, respect and revere the Hanging Judge and insist that all others accept his decisions without question.

During this time, far across the American continent, indeed as far as one may travel overland, the state of California was meeting the problem of lynch-executions in an entirely different manner, as radical in its way as that of the Free State. California's double lynching was in the best moving-picture tradition, a quickie that wrote its own scenario and was passed by a censorship board of the state's most distinguished citizens with only a few dissenters.

Thomas H. Thurmond confessed that he and John Holmes had kidnaped and murdered Brooke Hart, young San Jose businessman. It was a brutal affair; even a brief review of that part of the crime is revolting. Hart was snatched as he drove out of a parking lot on the evening of November 9. His abductors took him to the San Jose bridge, where they blindfolded him with a pillow slip, tied heavy cement blocks to his body, slugged him with a revolver, and shot him. They then threw him from the bridge and, observing his struggles in the water, fired half a dozen more shots into his body.

The kidnap-murderers proposed to collect a ransom of $40,000 from their victim's father, carrying on their negotiations almost entirely by telephone. The wires were tapped by the police, a trap was set, and Thurmond, on November 16, was taken into custody. His confession implicated Holmes, who was at once arrested, and both were incarcerated in the Santa Clara County jail to await trial. A reward of $500 for the recovery of Brooke Hart's body was offered by his father and, on November 26, two duck hunters found it in three feet of water in San Francisco Bay.

That night, as peaceful San Josans were returning

from the movies and theaters, they saw a mob composed of men, mostly young and on the hoodlum side, attack the county jail. The mob was repeatedly repulsed with tear bombs hurled by officers stationed about the building, and for a time the attack took the form of a siege. Then the leaders came forward to direct the mob's activities, and an eight-inch iron pipe was stripped from the partially completed San Jose post office adjoining the jail and used as a battering-ram. A second group, realizing the efficacy of the instrument, tore another pipe from the post office, and together the two crews battered their way into the jail. Sheriff Emig, who alone in San Jose seemed to know his duty, put up a stiff resistance but was so severely beaten that he was later taken to a hospital.

Once the mob was in the jail yard, there was no further resistance; police and guards were brushed aside. Thurmond and Holmes had been placed in separate cells on the second and third floors, and the mob divided to seize them. One group made a mistake and snatched the wrong prisoner; learning their error, they tossed him aside and returned for the right victim.

Word had spread all over the city, and by the time the mob brought their victims to the street, all San Jose was in a carnival spirit. The two kidnap-murderers were dragged a hundred yards to St. James

Park; Thurmond had fainted, but Holmes fought for his life every inch of the way. The unconscious man was hanged without difficulty and to the jeers of 6,000 spectators. Holmes was a powerful man, weighing above 200 pounds, and he put up a valiant struggle, fighting furiously. He was beaten down repeatedly, only to rise again, his body naked and bleeding. At last he was beneath the tree selected as his gallows and a rope was thrown around his neck; almost unconscious, he managed to throw it off. Again he was beaten down, and once more the noose was slipped about his throat, but he freed his hands and again threw it off. After a final beating, from which he did not revive, he was hauled fifteen feet into the air.

Six thousand San Josans applauded the hangings and 10,000 others, unable to get within sight of the lynchings, had to be content with adding their vocal approval. Men, women, and children enjoyed the barbaric spectacle as they would a circus. The San Jose police did their level best to help the affair to a successful climax by keeping out of the way and by permitting no one to enter St. James Park save the 6,000 already there. When the lynchings were completed, the police kept the crowds moving so that all might witness the bodies before they were humanely cut down.

Photographers were present, and many shots of the lynching and the lynchers were made; the actual lynchers could have been identified, arrested, and prosecuted. But for what purpose? Governor James Rolph, Jr., was no Governor Ritchie. Not by far. Governor Rolph must have had criminal knowledge of the proposed lynching, for he postponed a trip to Idaho to attend a conference of governors.

"*If I had gone away,*" said Rolph's statement, "*someone would have called out the troops on me, and I promised in Los Angeles I would not do that. Why should I call out the troops to protect those two fellows?*" [2]

Why, indeed? It's rather late to be inquiring. Governor Rolph has gone to his reward. The alleged spontaneity of the uprising, the flash of public indignation and outrage, seem to have been phony. It approaches criminal conspiracy if the Governor's words are to be taken literally. If he had gone away, someone would have called out the troops and then there would have been no lynching.

Earlier, Governor Rolph had said, even while the bodies of the lynched men were still warm: "This is the best lesson that California has ever given to the country."

[2] Italics are mine. F. S.

215

What is the worst lesson that California ever gave the country?

Later, when public-spirited Californians spoke of going over the Governor's head and seeking prosecution of the lynchers, Rolph came further to the aid of Judge Lynch: "If anyone is arrested for the good job, I'll pardon them all."

For several months it was touch-and-go between the pro-lynch Americans and their fellows opposed to the decisions of the incompetent judge. The pro-lynchers filled the columns of the daily papers with words of praise for the San Jose mob and for Governor Rolph, contemptuously referring to those who protested the outrage as "the right-minded." There was one hopeful sign in the fact there were so many right-minded, mostly outside California.

During these days while the Judge was traveling his circuit along the thirty-ninth parallel, the state of Missouri found another case requiring his attention. Approximately half way between Maryland and California, Missouri's Governor Park's method of handling his affair was approximately half way between that of Rolph and Ritchie. Park's method was what may be called the traditional one.

Lloyd Warner, a nineteen-year-old Negro, was

snatched from the county jail at St. Joseph and lynched on the courthouse lawn. This was the same jail in which Raymond Gunn had been confined for safekeeping in 1930; the same jail from which a mob that had come for Gunn was dispersed by the simple expedient of aiming an empty machine gun at it. Further, it may be recalled that Gunn was later moved to Kansas City for more safekeeping. Missouri, it would seem, does not retain very well; mobs learn from other mobs, but most peace officers apparently discontinue all mental development after securing their appointment.

On Tuesday, November 28, while the papers of the nation were featuring Governor Rolph's defense of lynching, Warner was arrested, charged with criminal assault on a twenty-one-year-old white girl on the previous Sunday night. His victim had been kicked and beaten and was found in a lonely alley bound with her own stockings. Only six months before Warner had narrowly escaped prosecution on a charge of assaulting a colored woman. When he was arraigned, he was ready, he said, to plead guilty. The Judge did not want to rush things and directed the case not be taken up until the next day.

Early that evening a mob began forming and expressed its intentions by hurling stones through the jail windows. Its members evidently had studied the

San Jose strategy and believed it effective. When
they were repulsed with tear gas, a small detachment
was sent for a five-inch iron pipe. The jail door resisted and, leadership failing to indicate the plan of
attack, the mob retired out of range. Governor Park
had time to order out a unit of the Missouri National
Guard, specifically the Thirty-fifth Tank Company,
with about sixty-five men.

"There appeared not to be time enough," said the
Governor, "to get National Guardsmen from other
towns nearby."

Recalling that a single guardsman with an empty
machine gun had dispersed the Maryville mob, one
might have thought sixty-five men with tanks would
have been enough.

The tanks rolled up to the county jail, and one tank
soldier who had failed to lock himself in was removed
from the machine by members of the mob and elimi-
nated from further participation. Then state highway
police were ordered to the scene. The mob had by
this time increased to such vast proportions that it
was too powerful. The tear gas bombs proved inef-
fectual, and hundreds of the mob crashed through the
doors of the jail and raced through the corridors. Officers within the jail hurled gas bombs indiscrimi-
nately, fist fights took place, and shots were fired;
then the forty officers melted before the mob, and the

prisoner was taken. The Negro, Warner, was a powerful man; he fought and kicked, and it took many members of the mob to quiet him. Subdued and stripped almost naked, the victim was dragged out by four young members of the mob, others who were following kicking and beating him. He was rushed to a tree about a block away, the mob cheering and shouting and cursing. Under the tree the Negro attempted to talk, but shouts of "string him up" drowned out whatever he said. He was pulled about eight feet into the air as the crowd cheered. Later the mob raided a nearby filling station, saturated the body with gasoline, and applied torches. When the rope by which the Negro was hanging parted, a fire was built about the body.

Later in Jefferson City, when told of the lynching, Governor Park said, "I have no comment to make."

However, four arrests were made. Two of the men were charged with first degree murder, one with possession of a pistol stolen from a guard on the night of the lynching, and the fourth with malicious destruction of property when the jail was attacked. There was none charged with simple obstruction of traffic. The four men were discharged the following year, after the failure of the jury to convict the one man against whom the State had the strongest case.

Thus three Governors in widely separated states

met Judge Lynch's incursions in varying ways; all of the Governors failed.

On December 5, President Roosevelt, speaking over a nationwide radio hook-up, condemned lynching and rebuked Governor Rolph, though he did not mention the California executive by name:

"This new generation, for example, is not content with preaching against that vile form of collective murder, lynch-law, which has broken out in our midst anew. We know that it is murder, and a deliberate and definite disobedience of the commandment, 'Thou shalt not kill.' We do not excuse those in high places or in low who condone lynch-law."

(H) Those Who Defied the Bosses

The United States, reputedly the most advanced of industrial nations, is probably the most backward in its attitude toward labor. Not only are the great industrialists themselves reactionary to the point of sheer feudalism, but they are backed up by a body of public opinion, vocal even if in the minority, that is ready to go to any lengths to preserve the present order. The basis of lynching Negroes in the South is obvious: the law of Judge Lynch is invoked to keep the black in his economic and cultural place. It is the unreconstructed South's answer to the Thirteenth Amendment; the southern Negro today is no less a helot than he was a century ago. This cruel weapon has also been found effective against white working men who, rising in protest against low wages and vile working conditions, threaten the profits of the dominant whites. The crack-pots of the Ku Klux Klan, the apostles of the rope and faggot, are at all times ready to put the Judge's bosses' edicts into effect.

The South is learning, somewhat belatedly, that it is a bad way to treat a low-priced labor market.

Short-sighted northern employers have long envied the South its control over its workers. They have sought to imitate the Klan and the Men of Justice with similar organizations. The Crusaders and the Sentinals of the Republic do not get down into the mud with their victims but they are equally repressive. The Black Legion and the Silver Shirts were ready to do any dirty work required of them so long as they could hide behind the flag. Failing to keep these groups secret, the employers have been compelled to institute their own lynch-law through company spies and company thugs. Instead of the death-penalty they use the yellow-dog contract, the shut-out and the blacklist, the Weir plan and the Mohawk Valley double-cross.

The northern employers have learned that all these repressive measures are ineffective against industrially organized workers. It is the workers in the jungles of industry, the unorganized and the poorly organized, those workers in whose minds the necessity for union is becoming apparent, who are the victims of these repressive measures.

When any of these workers attempt to organize, to form themselves into unions for collective strength and open bargaining, to protect their jobs and secure better working conditions, these underhanded employer-weapons fall upon them with a form of lynch-law. There are high motives that send priests and missionaries into savage lands, and the motives that take labor organizers into the jungles of industry are often no less exalted. They are missionaries of a better world. These missionaries, who seek to preach a better everyday life, are often met with violence and death, their temples wrecked, their leaders mobbed and beaten or jailed. When the police and laws have failed, when the workers become insistent upon remedial measures, the embattled industrialist summons his old ally, Judge Lynch, and his mob jury. Posters are thrown against walls announcing, "So and So Is Communistic. Communism Will Not Be Tolerated. Ku Klux Klan Rides Again."

Although Judge Lynch's white victims are not so numerous as his black sufferers of the same class, the whites would make an impressive total if any computation were possible. In labor wars the remains of the lynch-victims are often destroyed by burial in quick-lime, in phosphate pits, dropped into abandoned mines, or weighted down and thrown in rivers and harbors. Only on rare occasions are the bodies left to be found by the coroner; a lynched working man is propaganda too powerful for the masters.

Frank Little was lynched. So was Joe Hill, though the entire state of Utah and the Mormon Church had to get down in the mud to bring it about. Wesley Everest was barbarously mutilated before he was lynched. Frank Norman and Joseph Shoemaker were lynched. It isn't often that Judge Lynch wastes his time on cripples; not that he is too gallant to take advantage of women or the physically handicapped. Little was a barb in the crop of organized greed even if he hobbled on crutches.

Butte, Montana, has always been a wide open town for those with money. The bosses gambled and won with their profits and the workers lost. Speaking industrially, it has been called the city of gunmen and widows, of sweatholes and cemeteries. The sweatholes are the mines; they have been on fire for half a century, and the temperature averages about 116 degrees summer and winter. The fires are, officially, under control; it is only when the flame strikes a pocket of gas that things get messed up and some miners are picked up in grilled pieces and sent to their bereaved

223

families. The mine jobs are considered risky work, but there are many men in Butte who are happy to have the work. Sometimes conditions get so bad that even the most loyal workers are compelled to rebel.

On June 8, 1917, the aptly named Speculator Mine, one of Butte's most important, caught fire, and nearly two hundred miners were burned to death. Investigation showed that the Montana State Mining Law had been violated, that almost two hundred lives had been sacrificed for small profits. The solid concrete bulkheads separating the mines did not contain the required safety manholes. When the flames broke out, the workers swarmed to the lower levels, trying to find exits into other mines through the manholes. They found instead that the mine owners had saved some money by not putting them in, but the discovery cost them their lives. No mine operator was prosecuted for this violation of the law or for the deaths of the workers.

While the Speculator still stank of burned flesh, the miners went on strike, demanding not higher pay or shorter hours, but a higher safety standard. They didn't want to die while earning their pitiable wages in the sweatholes. The Industrial Workers of the World sent in Frank Little, a small, crippled fellow known from one end of the mining territory to the other as a capable organizer. Little had been beaten and had gone through as much persecution as it is possible for one man to stand; half-Indian, half-white, he did not seem to know the meaning of fear. That his efforts in organizing the miners in their fight for safety were effective there is no doubt. On the last day of July, 1917, he hobbled on his crutch to the cheap lodging house where he lived and went to his room. It had been a hard day and he discarded only his outer clothing and went to sleep. Some time during the night a gang of six men came and took him out, bound his hands behind his back, tied him to the rear of their car, and drove off into the night, dragging him through Butte streets. They literally tore off his kneecaps.

What happened after that is not known. The next morning Little's body was found hanging from a railroad trestle. It showed evidences of beating and had been mutilated. There was no police investigation. Frank Little was only a "wobbly," an enemy to those who could lose gracefully in Butte's gambling halls.

Little's case was not an isolated one. Other labor organizers were informed that they could expect the same treatment if they did not at once leave the city. They did not go; the strike continued for five months, when the workers, defeated by starvation, were forced back into the sweatholes.

What the workers in the outposts of industry, in the woods and mines, suffered during America's participation in the World War will never be known. Under the whiplash of the patriots, driven by the war-time need for immediate materials and the unparalleled opportunity for tremendous profits, many a rebellious worker was sent down the trail, *la longue traverse.*

The workers, once the Armistice was signed, resumed organizational activities. The patriots were through with their chauvinistic shouting and flag-waving; that curse was lifted. If the bosses had harbored any idea of recruiting returned veterans for their subversive tactics, they were sadly disillusioned, for only in isolated instances did the Legion permit itself to be used against the workers. The average Legionnaire soon realized that in any battles at home he belonged on the side of his fellow workers.

Centralia was an exception.

Calling names never does much harm to either opponent in a quarrel, no matter how apt the epithets happen to be. When the union lumber-workers referred to the lumber interests as the "timber beast," the beast retaliated with "timber wolves." The appellations were well deserved, and it was only when the stronger "beast" began exterminating the "wolves" that war was declared. And the beast showed how beastly it could be, and the wolves proved to be only so many rabbits, though of a lion-hearted variety.

In most of the various warring nations the soldiers who were fortunate enough to survive returned to their home towns and became a part of the civilian population, changing their uniforms for mufti and, save for a small star in their lapels, becoming indistinguishable from their non-combatant fellows. In America, the returned veteran, whether he had been to the battlefields or only to a camp, became a sort of demigod. His person, his welfare, and his future became the deep concern of the patriots and of the Government. Nothing was too good for our brave heroes. They had founded a veteran-organization before they left France, and no one protested, though such an organization might have wielded, under certain conditions, a greater influence for evil than the Ku Klux Klan. The veteran-organization prospered and thrived where labor unions failed. Many towns and cities gave their units small endowments, rent-free quarters, and many other considerations.

It was something of a shock to the people who had so glorified the veterans to learn that on the first anniversary of their victory four of them had been shot down in cold blood by members of a subversive body known as the I.W.W. On November 11, 1919, the Legionnaires of Centralia, Washington, had donned their old uniforms and gone forth to parade the streets, to celebrate their victory, and to honor the memory of those fellows-at-arms who had not returned. It was a memorial service that was being repeated in every town and city in the land; in the minds of most Americans the victims might have been their own boys in their own home town. That was the way it read in the papers, in the indignant editorials and in the letters to the editors.

But the story did not begin and end on that November 11, but went away back to 1912, when the beasts and the wolves started calling each other names.

Armistice Day parades follow a definite program. The participants assemble at a predetermined point, the band strikes up, and the parade moves over a known route, past a reviewing stand and on to the dispersal point. In some parades, unloaded or dummy rifles are carried by all the participants; in others, only the color guard or the guard of honor carry rifles loaded with blank cartridges. The parade is a peacetime demonstration.

In no Armistice Day parades are ropes carried nor are certain leaders armed with loaded revolvers.

In 1918, the patriots of Centralia, as a war-time measure, had raided and closed the hall of the local

Industrial Workers of the World. They were not entirely a destructive mob; they demolished only what
they could not use elsewhere. Desks, chairs, and type-
writers went to true-blue patriots, and the local's
phonograph was auctioned off for the benefit of the
Red Cross. The only Wobbly in sight, a blind news-
paperman, was taken for a ride, tossed out into a
ditch, and warned not to return. The raid was successful in a way; the patriots were rid of some of the
wolves, they thought, and in their simple way had
helped make the world safe for democracy. The chief
drawback was that the Wobblies secured more desks,
chairs, and a typewriter and re-opened their headquarters almost immediately. Business went on as
usual; the literature put out to incite the wolves only
incited the beast to violence against the union.

In 1919 the I.W.W. had organized a strike in the
short log country of eastern Washington and, in
dread that the strike would spread westward, the
western Washington lumber owners decided that the
unions must be driven out for all time. A meeting,
advertised frankly to achieve this purpose, was held
in the Elks' lodge rooms in Centralia. After eighteen
years, the evidence is practically conclusive that the
Legion, as an organization, was not a party to the plan
but the tool of certain influential citizens, some of
them members of the local post. The 1918 raid had

been conducted under cover of a Red Cross parade; the 1919 affair would be covered by the Armistice Day services. The idea was to "let the men in uniform do it."

The parade formed and passed down the main street; it did not stop at the designated dispersal place, but at the command of armed leaders continued for several blocks, past the I.W.W. union hall for another block. Then, again defying parade customs, it turned in its tracks and made its way back to the union hall. As the Legionnaires of Centralia came abreast of the building, a leader shouted the usual command: "Let's go!" and some of the paraders broke ranks and charged the union headquarters.

The proposed raid was no secret in Centralia. The Wobblies knew it was coming—had, in fact, secured legal advice that they would be within their rights in protecting their property. As the glass of their windows crashed and armed men began entering their hall, they let go a burst of gunfire. One of the leaders of the paraders, Warren Grimm, was shot in the abdomen, and before he died, he said: "It serves me right. I had no business there." Others were wounded, and during the lull occasioned by the shock, the Wobblies retreated through back doors and windows.

Many of the Wobblies, it may be remembered, were veterans themselves. One of these, Wesley Everest, was armed with a forty-five caliber automatic, and it is believed that his shots had killed Grimm and another veteran, Arthur McElfresh. With his pocket full of cartridges, Everest retreated, shooting. He would run a hundred yards, followed by the mob, turn and shoot. The mob would stop with him and resume running when he ran. He was cornered at a river bank, made his last stand, and, in self-defense, shot and killed Dale Hubbard, a nephew of one of the lumber owners.

"Stand back," he shouted, brandishing his automatic. "If there are any bulls in the crowd, I'll submit to arrest."

The mob closed in on him, and it was then learned what the ropes that had been carried in the parade were for.

"Let's finish the job," said a voice.

"You haven't got guts enough to lynch a man in the daytime," was Everest's defiant comment.

The rope was placed around his neck, but the cries to swing him up were interrupted by a woman who brushed through the crowd and threw the rope from his neck.

"You are curs and cowards to treat a man like that!"

Everest had been shot in the side; he was taken not to a hospital but to the city jail, where he was thrown into the bull pen. There he lay in a wet heap on the

231

cement floor, twitching in agony, only an occasional moan escaping his lips.

That night the lights of Centralia were shut off, and under cover of darkness members of the mob went to the jail and took the semi-conscious Wesley Everest out. They had no trouble finding him; a guard called through the darkness:

"Don't shoot, men! Here is your man."

Everest knew why the mob had come. He staggered to his feet defiantly and, as the mob dragged him through the corridor, he shouted:

"Tell the boys I died for my class."

He was thrown into the back of an automobile, pushed to the floor, and hurried to the Chehalis River bridge. Before they reached their destination the hands of his captors were sticky and red, their trousers sodden with the blood of their captive. One had reached into his pocket, brought out a razor, and for a moment fumbled over the body on the floor. Suddenly there was a piercing scream and Everest cried:

"For Christ's sake, men, shoot me! Don't let me suffer like this!"

The man with the razor finished his work. The car sped on to the bridge, where the men hanged him, not once but three times. As they lowered him over the side of the bridge, his hands convulsively clutched the planking, and one stamped on the fingers until the hold was broken. Then they hoisted him up and hanged him again and again. The sadistic affair was not yet over; flashlights were played upon the hanging body, and volley after volley of bullets was pumped into it.

The next morning a member of the lynch mob went among his fellow-lynchers and advised them:

"We've got to get that body or the Wobs will find it and raise hell over its condition."

The coroner's report on the death of Wesley Everest was not delivered officially to the people of Centralia. It was delivered a few nights later at the Elks' Club.

"Everest," he stated, "broke out of jail, went to the Chehalis Bridge, and hanged himself. Finding the rope too short, he climbed back and, fastening on a longer one, jumped off again."

Whereas the Negro is the chief whipping-boy below Mason and Dixon's Line, the white working man who has the temerity to stick his neck out is quite likely to find a noosed rope about it when he draws it back. There are definite things the dominant whites cannot tolerate: Negroes who refuse to stay in the place assigned to them; white workers who protest the conditions imposed upon them; anyone

233

who questions the voice that constantly intones the chant: "We know how to run this part of the country."

When they are unable to corrupt their courts of law, they go to a higher authority. They call in the Klan. The White Legion. The Men of Justice. *Judge Lynch.*

Although workers in any part of these United States are subject to repressive measures, the chief centers of repression are in the South. Harlan County, Kentucky coal mining area, is infamous for its flouting of civil liberties; conditions in eastern Arkansas among the farm and cotton sharecroppers are a stench in the nostrils of all Americans; the Vigilantes have spattered the fruit and vegetables of southern California with the blood of American and Mexican workers. In Atlanta, Birmingham, and New Orleans one has only to be denounced as a Red or a Communist to have a mob of red-baiters on his heels. Number One sore spot is Tampa, Florida.

Tampa is noted for its cigars, but cigar-making is the city's third largest industry. It is the center of a citrus-growing country, and an almost steady stream of oranges, grapefruit, and sub-tropical vegetables passes through the seaport; yet the citrus industry is not Tampa's greatest. The fifteen- to twenty-million-dollars-a-year industry, the all-year crop, is gambling. In Tampa the dominant whites are Klansmen, leaders who use the rank and file of members to hold their positions. The citizens of Tampa differ not at all from the citizens of any other American city; they choose their mayors and city officials by ballot, the police are appointed and patrol the streets, the tax-gatherers are just as insistent as anywhere else. Yet the city is Klan dominated. It is said that it is useless to seek appointment to the police or fire department unless you are a Klan member. If a Klan member commits a crime, it is difficult to secure an arrest, and it is said that if the Klan does not care for you, your house may burn for all the fire department cares.

A few citizens, working men for the most part, deplored the situation and thought that something should be done to correct it. In 1935, as always, there was only the dominant Democratic party, and a professed Republican was no better than an alien. As a matter of policy, these protesting citizens decided to call their new party the Modern Democrats and, because some of them were former Socialists, the Klan-dominated opposition charged them as communists. The Klan did not don their nightshirts and go after the Modern Democrats; they were fearless and kept on their police uniforms and plain clothes and did it all according to the book.

In a democracy such as ours any individual or group has a right to fight, obeying all legal rules, any other individual or group. If the Ku Klux Klan decides to fight communism, it is well within its rights; it may fight tooth and nail and no holds barred. The Communist party has a right to battle the Klan and its fascist implications under the same terms. But the issues and terms should be clearly defined: the Klan may not pursue its own subversive activities by merely labeling anything to which it is opposed as communism. But reason is too rare and beautiful an impulse to expect from a Klansman.

"All things," says the Klan Kreed, "and matters which do not exist within this Order or are not authorized by or do not come under its jurisdiction shall be designated as the 'Alien World.' All persons who are not members of this Order shall be designated as 'Aliens.' "

The men who organized the Modern Democrats were anything but communists: a few had been Socialists, most were industrious working men, all the organizers were union members. It is known now that many of the citizens of Tampa were sympathetic to their movement, but if they were permitted to continue they would become a menace to the Klan-machine.

One evening six of them were to meet in execu-tive session. Seated about the living-room table in the home of Mrs. A. M. Herald, they were debating the form their constitution should take and had decided to pattern it after that of the American Legion. They were Joseph Shoemaker, chairman, formerly a mem-ber of the S.P.; Sam Rogers, WPA worker, an M.D. from Loyola College; Walter Roush, president of the Sulphur Springs Workers Alliance and a member of the S.P.; Charles E. Jensen, a member of the S.P.; and J. A. McCaskill, a Tampa fireman whose father was a Tampa policeman. The sixth man, who had not yet appeared, was Eugene F. Poulnot, formerly presi-dent of the Pressmen's Union, A.F. of L., then a WPA worker and chairman of the Florida Workers' Alliance. McCaskill offered to go after him.

As soon as Poulnot stepped inside the house, seven policemen entered; three came in the front door and four in the back. Guns were drawn, papers grabbed, and the men were searched. Six men were arrested, but only the names of five appeared on the police blotter; the name of J. A. McCaskill was missing. They were taken to police headquarters and grilled. Later they were released, not in a group, but one by one. As they left headquarters, they were snatched, one

by one, and shoved into cars and taken to the woods.
When Poulnot struggled and fought against being
taken into the automobile, a crowd gathered. One of
the kidnapers announced:

"We're taking a crazy man to Chattahoochee."

Shoemaker was tumbled in on top of Poulnot and
the car hurried to a point fourteen miles outside
Tampa. Rogers was taken in another car. For some
reason Roush and Jensen were not beaten, but were
permitted to return to their homes. Rogers was
stripped and placed over a log. His hands and feet
were held while he was beaten. Then boiling tar was
applied to his abdomen, sexual organs, and thighs.

Shoemaker and Poulnot suffered even worse. Poulnot was flogged with a chain and a rawhide, then he
was tarred and feathered. Once, as he revived, one of
his lynchers said: "The —— is faking. Let's give it
to him!"

The tortures that Shoemaker went through will
never be known. He was too horribly mutilated ever
to tell. That he suffered more than Poulnot is evident. The boiling tar had been poured over his naked
body and burned into his lacerated flesh. For seven
hours he lay beside the road, unconscious through a
night suddenly turned cold. At the Centro Español
Hospital, to which he was taken, it was possible to

warm him only with hot water bottles. A leading Tampa surgeon examined him and stated:

"He was horribly mutilated. I wouldn't beat a hog the way that man was whipped. He was beaten until he was paralyzed on one side, probably from blows on the head. He cannot say anything to you; he does not know what happened. He cannot use one arm, and I doubt if three square feet would cover the total area of bloodshot bruises on his body, not counting the parts injured only by tar."

For days Joseph Shoemaker lingered between life and death, suffering terrible agonies. In a final, desperate attempt to save his life, one of his legs was amputated. On the ninth day he died.

The people of Tampa were aroused. On December 12, three days after Shoemaker's death, the Tampa *Tribune* stated: "The state investigators have found evidence that leads them to believe Shoemaker and the others were framed." Such a public admission of police guilt was unexpected in Tampa. News of the outrage had spread throughout the country, and the Klan-police knew they had overshot their mark. Policemen were warned not to talk. Police Chief Tittsworth, devoting all his activities to covering up the evidence of the crime, found himself indicted as an accessory after the fact. Local public indignation, backed by Tampa newspapers, was strong, and indictments followed on charges of kidnaping and murder. How great was the power of the Klan was seen in the indictments, which were loosely worded and provided many legal loop-holes. Still the Klan was thoroughly frightened, how frightened may be guessed from the fact that the *Klan strategists asked for a change of venue.*

It was known that the same men who had beaten E. F. Poulnot were the murderers of Joseph Shoemaker, yet they were placed on trial charged with the kidnaping only of Poulnot. Governor Dave Sholtz designated Judge Robert T. Dewell to hear the case, and the trial was moved to Bartow, in Polk County, on the ground that the Klansmen-police-defendants could not hope for a fair hearing in Tampa. The main defense argument was that the victims were communists and therefore not entitled to the protection of the law. The trial was marked by the Judge's sympathy for the defendants to such an extent that the Court rallied to the defense attorney's argument that unless the *sole intent* of the kidnaping was to confine the victim secretly, the jury could not convict. Here the honorable Judge's own words of instruction to the jury:

"Even if you are satisfied from the evidence be-

yond and to the exclusion of every reasonable doubt
that the defendants, without lawful authority, seized
the said E. F. Poulnot and illegally and unlawfully
carried him from the City Hall to the Estuary, and
there turned him over to other persons, who in turn
carried him into the country and flogged the said E. F.
Poulnot, you still could not convict the defendants
unless you believe beyond every reasonable doubt
that it was their intention to secretly confine or im-
prison the said E. F. Poulnot."

But the jury disagreed with His Honor. Made up
of working men, it brought in a verdict of guilty.
The jurors later told newspapermen that they had
been unanimous on the first ballot.

The Klan was not beaten, not yet through. The
convicted Klansmen were given sentences of four
years, though under the law they could have been
condemned to serve ten years. Even at that, they did
not go to jail, but were sent to their homes under
bond, pending disposition of their appeal in the Supreme Court of Florida.

The Klan brought their heavy guns into action.
The best lawyers searched the records for precedents,
the finest attorneys sent their briefs to the highest
court in the state and came away with a reversal of
the convictions on the ground that Judge Dewell

committed an error in permitting the introduction of evidence concerning a conspiracy on the part of the defendants to commit the crime of kidnaping.

The new trial was held in October, 1937, almost two years after the flogging, the criminal assault, if you insist, and the defendants, again before Judge Dewell, were acquitted.

Earlier, the Klan decided their members would not be put on trial for the murder of Joseph Shoemaker. When State's Attorney Rex Farrior appeared before Judge Dewell to have the date fixed for the murder case, the Court announced that no trial of the homicide case would be allowed because *the state had failed to pay Polk County the sum of $531.60, expenses incurred for bailiff fees and the like in the Poulnot case.*

Public-spirited citizens became indignant and hastened to contribute the money owed Polk County so that the eleven men who were indicted for murder might be brought to trial. Somewhat reluctantly, Judge Dewell set the murder trial for April 19, 1937, later removing it from the calendar; he gave as his reasons the failure, at that time, of the higher court to pass on the appeal of the five men convicted of kidnaping. Even to a layman it must be apparent that the murder of Shoemaker had nothing to do with the conviction of the men who flogged Poulnot. The

Klan works in mysterious ways its wonders to perform.

The Florida Klan has a better plan than lynching to be rid of those they label communistic: it is mysterious disappearance with no traces left. Frank Norman was an organizer of the United Citrus Workers' Union and a thorn in the side of the dominant whites. One of his aims was that blacks and whites should stick together, each refusing to scab on the other. It was bad enough to try to organize the white fruit pickers, but to urge them to stand together with Negroes was too much.

There was a knock on the door of the Lakeland home of Frank Norman, and he answered it to learn that three men, calling themselves Sheriff Chase and two deputies, wanted him to go down the road toward Haines City to identify a Negro who had been lynched. They said that Norman's name had been found in the victim's pocket.

Mrs. Norman wanted to go with him but was dissuaded: instead, a friend, Ben Surrency, went with Norman to the Sheriff's car. Mr. Surrency was the last friend to see Frank Norman:

"Mr. Norman stepped in the car in the rear seat; I followed in the middle. The supposed Mr. Chase got in with us in the back seat. As we drove off a possible one

243

hundred yards from the house, Mr. Norman asked Mr. Chase to show his authority as he did not know whether he was the high sheriff or not. The man answered, 'I am not Sheriff Chase, but a deputy from Highland City. It doesn't matter; the Negro has a card with your name and home address on it, and we want you to identify him so we can take him down for an inquest.' Mr. Norman says, 'Will you please stop about one hundred yards farther down the road so I can pick up another man, as he might be a help to identify the Negro?' The man says, 'Sure,' and turned on Ingram Avenue instead of following the Bartow Road according to Mr. Norman's instructions. I judge we drove forty yards when the car came to a sudden stop. The man sitting beside the driver covered Mr. Norman with a gun. Then he asked me my name. As I told him my name was Ben Surrency, he said, 'Get out. I don't want you.' I got out as I was told. Mr. Norman put up both his hands, asking the man what in the world does this mean. Mr. Norman was saying other words as I was rushed out of the car and I could not understand what he was saying. As I got on the street a gun fired. And an awful thumping noise was heard in the car. The supposed-to-be Sheriff Chase took me by the shoulder and faced me back home and told me not to look. Another car forty or fifty feet back of the car I just got out of and facing me stopped with their bright lights on. Both cars remained still until I had passed the second car some distance. Then they both sped on."

Frank Norman did not return. Nor has his body been discovered. It may have been buried in an un-

known grave, or burned in a mysterious fire that occurred a few days later. It may have been weighted
and sunk in one of the many lakes in the vicinity, or
dropped into one of the flooded phosphate pits
close by.

Frank Norman's fellow-workers know who was
behind his murder and they were not astonished at
the apathetic investigation. No one could expect the
Klan to go around to the courthouse to indict itself.

(1) *1937*

Politely ignoring the records in a burst of gubernatorial pride on April 13 of last year, Governor
Hugh White of Mississippi announced in an address
before the Farm Chemurgic Conference at Jackson
that the state had not had a lynching in fifteen months.
The Governor was wrong: the records show that
just four months before his declaration, J. B. Grant,
seventeen-year-old Negro, of Laurel, was shot to
death by a mob. After his body had been riddled with
more than a hundred bullets, it was tied to an automobile and dragged through the streets, then hanged
to a trestle. Governor White can read the whole story
in the Memphis (Tennessee) *Press-Scimitar* for December 5. Even at that, we can forgive the Governor
his moment of pride, for in the year 1935 his state

had got right down in the mud with a credit of eight
of the total of twenty-five lynchings for the year.

But even as the Governor left the platform he was
given the news that, while he was speaking, two Negroes were being lynched in the state of Mississippi.

Only eight men were lynched in 1937; all were
colored, and only one was accused of a sexual crime.
All the lynchings were confined to what is known as
the lynch-belt, and all followed the constant pattern
of the years. There were two double lynchings, one
while Congress was debating the Gavagan Bill; a
brand new method in torture was introduced; one
Negro lynched was innocent of any crime and was
thrown by the Sheriff as a sop to the mob. One was
lynched by a mob seeking another.

In Alabama, at Abbeyville, on February 2, Wesley
Johnson, twenty-two, was taken from the Henry
County jail by a mob of a hundred men. He was
charged with attempted assault and was taken to the
scene of the alleged crime and riddled with bullets.
Later Attorney-General A. A. Carmichael asserted
he could prove conclusively that Johnson was innocent of the crime, that the Sheriff knew he was innocent, but made the arrest to appease the populace.

There were no arrests, though impeachment proceedings against the Sheriff were instituted, and no convictions.

At Duck Hill, Mississippi, April 13, two Negroes accused of the murder of a country merchant on December 30, 1936, were snatched by twelve men from the Sheriff and two deputies as they were being returned to jail. "Boot Jack" MacDaniels and Roosevelt Townes, the victims, were hurried to the scene of their crime, stripped to the waist, and chained to trees. A member of the mob brought out a gasoline blow-torch. The torch flames were sprayed on the Negroes' bared breasts and they were ordered to confess. MacDaniels was the first to feel the searing blow-torch and readily confessed that he had robbed the merchant after Townes had killed him. He was then riddled with bullets. Townes, the Associated Press reported, died under the torture of the blow-torch. Both men in their confessions implicated another man, who was later captured and brought to the carnival. The third man admitted he had originally been a party to the conspiracy but insisted he had withdrawn before the crime. He was severely beaten and ordered to leave the state. The lynch mob, assisted by the hundred spectators, piled brush high about the victims and burned their bodies. Governor

White was reported "outraged," but even at that there were no arrests, no indictments, and no convictions.

On July 20, Judge Lynch went to Tallahassee, Florida, and snatched Richard Hawkins and Ernest Ponder, two young Negroes charged with stabbing a policeman, from a jail but two blocks away from the Florida capitol. They were taken three miles over the Tallahassee-Jacksonville highway and hanged. There were no investigations, no arrests, no indictments, and no convictions. On August 27, the St. Petersburg *Times* commented:

"An investigation into the lynching of two Negroes in Tallahassee got nowhere, just as everyone, familiar with Florida justice, expected."

Just about the time that Florida's state capital was enjoying its double lynching, Tennesseeans were smugly telling themselves that it couldn't happen in Tennessee. On July 19, Sheriff Vaughan outraced a mob that had formed to lynch Albert Gooden, charged with murder, and got his man to Memphis for safekeeping. The state was getting credit for a prevented lynching when the Sheriff went to bring Gooden back to the Marion jail. The Sheriff, it seems, brought the prisoner direct to the waiting mob and delivered him without any protest. Something had happened in the meantime. The Sheriff had been put on the spot and did his level best to recapture his popular standing with the lynch-minded. There were but six members in the mob that on August 17 took Gooden away from the peace officer, rushed him to a railroad trestle near Covington, hanged him, and riddled his body with bullets. There were no arrests, no indictments, and, consequently, no convictions.

On September 3, at Mount Vernon, Georgia, a small mob, engaged in a man-hunt for a Negro accused of assaulting a white woman, desired to search the home of Will Kirby, Negro. Kirby resisted and was shot and killed by the mob. The state of Georgia indicated by its lack of action in the matter that it would like to forget the whole affair.

Until October 4, Florida was tied with its old rival, Mississippi, for the 1937 lynch-dishonors. On that day a Crestview mob snatched J. C. Evans, charged with robbery and a "crime against nature" involving a twelve-year-old boy, from the Sheriff and riddled his body with buckshot and pistol bullets. In commenting on the three lynchings in Florida this year, the Miami *News* stated:

"In each case, prisoners have been seized from what appeared to be careless and inadequately manned guards. The circumstances in more than one case even left room for hints of collusion between mobsters and officers of the law. In each case a 'thorough' investigation has been promised and in each case up to the present, the investigators were quite unable to 'establish the identity' of the murderers."

Score: Florida 3; Mississippi 2; Alabama 1; Georgia 1; Tennessee 1.

The total membership of all lynch mobs for the year was under five hundred; the number of peace officers unfaithful to their vows was but seven. This small number of criminals has put the lynch-curse on the rest of the one hundred and twenty-five million Americans and held us up to the contempt and scorn of all civilized peoples.

Chapter Seven

THE REVERSALS OF JUDGE LYNCH

As a nation we have been conditioned to the lynch-spirit. Throughout our lives we shout our disapproval of baseball decisions and demand that the umpire be killed. When we meet with a new type of criminal, or when one of us proposes a too-radical public course, we assure one another that the offender should be taken out and strung up to the nearest telegraph pole. Lynch-spirit is not the monopoly of the South; it is firmly fixed in our national psychology. Much of our collective thinking ends in thoughts of violence.

There is but one effective curb on the activities of the Hanging Judge, and that is an awakened public consciousness of the evil. Lynchings do not happen where the people do not want them. Peace officers are human; they are politicians dependent upon popular support for continuance in office; they give their people what they want. Crime in any form must be tolerated to exist. As a people, we may not entirely approve lynch-executions, but we do tolerate them. An extended educational program might correct this fault, but it would be a long and costly process, costly in the lives that would be destroyed while the program was being brought to a conclusion.

With public opinion failing to end the lynch-spirit, dependence must be placed upon better peace officers and upon the enactment of more stringent laws. Since the Armistice, twice as many threatened lynchings have been prevented as have been consummated. But a frustrated lynch mob is as much an expression of the lynch-spirit as a successful lynching. Lives have been saved through the resourcefulness of the peace officers, and would-be lynchers have been prevented from becoming actual murderers. That the list of frustrated lynchings increases annually is a matter for satisfaction.[1]

Most lynchings occur either soon after the commission of the crime, when the criminal has been arrested, or later, when he is to be brought before the court. The earlier mob can usually be handled by resolute peace officers. It is the later mob, more deliberate and better organized, that is the more dangerous. The lynch leaders, having determined upon a lynching, survey the situation and make their plans

[1]

1919....43	1924....61	1929....34	1934....74
1920....84	1925....53	1930....60	1935....84
1921...108	1926....40	1931....91	1936....79
1922...114	1927....68	1932....43	1937....56
1923....56	1928....40	1933....48	

Source: *Negro Year Book,* 1937–1938.

strategically. Against such mobs there must be the use of legal and official strategy. The weapons are available in almost every state, and the competent peace officer should know how to use them effectively. The prisoner may be sent to another and stronger jail for safekeeping; a stronger and more effective guard accompanies him to and from the court; the state police and the militia may be called for further protection of the prisoner. Finally, many states provide for a change of venue.

Mobs must be broken up by the use of force. Any sheriff worthy of his office is aware of the awakening of the mob-spirit, and immediate action can be made effective. The actual leaders can be determined and arrested before the lynching. The forces of the law are and must always be kept stronger than those of the lawless. In 1934, at Shelbyville, Tennessee, in a county conditioned to lynching, a lynch mob was repulsed by state troops who killed three and wounded twenty mob members. The intended victim was saved, though the mob did burn the courthouse. In Sherman, Texas, the lynch-victim could have been saved by a similar show of force. Had Henry Lowry been conducted to jail as the Governor instructed, he would have paid the legal penalty for his crime instead of the lynch-penalty. Dr. Raper reports a Texas case where the Sheriff sought out the man who was or-

ganizing a lynching and nipped the affair in the bud
by delivering the leader a hefty blow that knocked
him off his feet.

Most legislation relating to lynching is punitive,
and some of it is prophylactic. The great body of such
laws are designed for the protection of intended
lynch-victims who are already in the hands of the
law. The chief need is for the protection against lynching of a person not yet arrested.

"Lynching has no technical legal meaning. It is
merely a descriptive phrase used to signify the lawless
acts of persons who violate established law at the
time they commit the acts. . . . The offense of
lynching is unknown to the common law." [2]

Some states have defined lynching and made it a
crime: Alabama, Indiana, Kansas, Kentucky, Virginia,
and North Carolina. Georgia has made lynching a
statutory crime, but without defining it. Other states
have defined mob-violence and made it a crime: Illinois, Pennsylvania, New Jersey, and West Virginia.
Of the ten states having statutory definitions of the
crime of lynching or mob violence, seven have had

[2] *Corpus Juris*, Vol. XXXVIII, 328. Quoted from Chadbourn: *Lynching and the Law.*

lynchings since the respective enactments: Alabama,
17; Illinois, 8; Kansas, 5; Kentucky, 8; North Carolina,
38; Virginia 1; West Virginia, 1.

ALABAMA: Any number of persons assembled for
any unlawful purpose and intending to injure any
person by violence and without authority of the law
shall be regarded as a mob, and any act of violence
exercised by such a mob upon the body of any person shall, when such act results in the death of the
injured person, constitute the crime of lynching; and
any person who participates in or actively aids or
abets such lynching shall, on conviction, suffer death
or be imprisoned in the penitentiary for not less than
five years, at the discretion of the jury; and any person, who, being a member of any such mob and
present at any such lynching, shall not actively
participate in the lynching, shall be deemed guilty of
abetting such lynching, and, on conviction, shall be
imprisoned for not less than one year nor more than
twenty-one years, at the discretion of the jury.

Any Sheriff, deputy sheriff, or jailer who negli-
gently or through cowardice, allows a prisoner to
be taken from the jail of his county, or to be taken
from his custody and put to death by violence, or to
receive bodily harm, must, on conviction, be fined
not less than $500 or more than $2,000, and may

also be sentenced to hard labor for the county for not more than two years.

No provisions are made for the liability of a city or county for mob violence causing personal or property damages.

ARIZONA: No anti-lynching legislation.

ARKANSAS: No anti-lynching legislation. Change of venue and special court terms to avoid mob violence in cases involving rape, murder, etc.

CALIFORNIA: No anti-lynching legislation. Every county and municipal corporation is responsible for injury to real or personal property within its corporate limits, done or caused by mobs or riots.

COLORADO: No anti-lynching legislation.

CONNECTICUT: No anti-lynching legislation. City or borough responsible for all injuries to person and property, including injuries causing death, when such injuries are caused by an act of violence of any person or persons while a member of, or acting in concert with, any assembly of persons engaged in disturbing the public peace, provided such city or borough or the police or other proper authorities thereof shall not have exercised reasonable care or diligence in the prevention or suppression of such mob, riotous assembly, or assembly engaged in disturbing the public peace.

DELAWARE: No anti-lynching legislation.

FLORIDA: No anti-lynching legislation. Law provides for change of venue on the order of the Governor.

GEORGIA: "And if the evidence submitted shall reasonably show that there is probability or danger of lynching, or other violence, then it shall be mandatory on said judge to change the venue to such a county in the State, as, in his judgment, will avoid such lynching.

". . . . and any person so engaged in mobbing or lynching any citizen of this State without due process shall be punished by imprisonment in the penitentiary for not less than one nor more than twenty years, and should death result from such mob violence, then the prisoner causing such death shall be subject to indictment and trial for the offense of murder."

IDAHO: No anti-lynching legislation. Law provides for change of jail and employment of a guard.

ILLINOIS: Defines a mob: that any collection of individuals, five or more in number, assembled for the unlawful purpose of offering violence to the person or property of anyone supposed to have been guilty of a violation of the law, or for the purpose of exercising correctional powers or regulative powers over any person or persons by violence, and without lawful authority, shall be regarded and designated as a "mob."

Any person or persons who shall compose a mob, with the intent to inflict damage or injury to the person or property of any individual charged with a crime, or, under the pretense of exercising correctional powers over such person or persons by violence, and without authority of the law, shall be subject to a fine of not less than $100 or more than $1,000, and may be imprisoned in the county jail not less than thirty days nor to exceed twelve months for each offense. In case the person or persons composing the mob commit injury to a person or damage to property they shall be deemed guilty of a felony and suffer imprisonment in the penitentiary not exceeding five years.

In the case of the death of the victim, the surviving spouse, lineal heirs, or adopted children may recover from such county or city damages for injuries sustained by reason of the loss of life of such person a sum not exceeding $5,000. Damage to property by mobs may be collected from the county or city to an amount not exceeding $5,000.

The loss by a Sheriff of his prisoner to a lynch mob is to be considered *prima facie* evidence of failure to do his duty, and he may be removed by the Governor. The law also enables the Sheriff to remove any pris-

oner in danger of lynching to another county for
safekeeping.

INDIANA: Lynching and mob clearly defined. Any
number of persons assembled for any unlawful purpose and intending to injure any person by violence
and without authority of the law shall be regarded as
a mob, and any act of violence exercised by such mob
upon the body of a person shall, when such act results
in the death of the injured person, constitute the
crime of lynching; and any person who participates
in or actively aids or abets such lynching shall, on
conviction, suffer death or be imprisoned in the state
prison during life; and any person who, being present
at any such lynching, shall not actively participate
in the lynching shall be deemed guilty of abetting
such lynching, and, on conviction, shall be imprisoned in the state prison for not less than two years
nor more than twenty-one years.

The law further provides complete protection for
the Sheriff and his prisoner who is threatened with
lynching. The prisoner may be sent to another county,
the Sheriff may "command all bystanders and others
with whom he can directly communicate to aid and
assist in defending such prisoner," and he may appeal
directly to the Governor for further aid by the state's
military forces. Failure to use all the weapons placed
at his command and losing his prisoner to the mob

shall be considered *prima facie* evidence of failure of official duty and result in removal and a fine of not more than $1,000.

The law, however, makes no provision for liability of city or county for personal or property damage.

IOWA: No anti-lynching legislation.

KANSAS: Any collection of individuals assembled for an unlawful purpose, intending to injure any person by violence, and without authority of law, shall for the purpose of this act be regarded as a "mob," and any act of violence exercised by such mob upon the body of any person shall constitute the crime of "lynching" when such act or acts of violence result in death; and any person who participates in or aids or abets such lynching, upon conviction thereof, shall be imprisoned in the state prison for not less than five years or during life, in the discretion of the jury.

The law further provides that anyone who harbors, conceals, or assists any lyncher to escape arrest shall be deemed an accessory after the fact, and upon conviction be imprisoned from for two to twenty-one years. Complete protection for the Sheriff and his prisoner who is threatened with lynching is part of the law: the prisoner may be transferred to a state prison or reformatory, the peace officer may command all bystanders and others with whom he can directly communicate to aid and assist in defending such prisoner, and he may call upon the Governor for the aid of the state's military forces. Failure to use the legal weapons provided will be considered sufficient cause for his removal from office by the Governor, and a Sheriff so renounced shall not be eligible to either election or appointment to the office. Liability of the city or county for personal or property damage is provided.

KENTUCKY: Any number of persons more than three, assembled for the purpose of doing violence or injury to, or for lynching, any person in custody of any peace officer or jailer in this Commonwealth shall be regarded as a mob. Any person who takes part in and with any such mob, with the result that the person in custody meets death at the hands of any such mob, shall be deemed guilty of lynching; or if the result be that the person does not meet death, any person who takes part in or with the mob shall be guilty of attempted lynching. The penalty for lynching shall be death or life imprisonment. The penalty for attempted lynching shall be confinement in the penitentiary for not less than two years or more than twenty-one years.

The law provides the peace officer with legal weapons for the full protection of any prisoner threatened with lynching and provides for his removal from office. Provision is also made for the liability of the city for property damage if preventable.

LOUISIANA: No anti-lynching legislation. Law provides that a prisoner may be removed for safekeeping.

MAINE: No anti-lynching legislation. Law provides that prisoner may be removed when jail is adjudged unfit or insecure. Liability of town for property damage limited to three fourths of damage done.

MARYLAND: No anti-lynching legislation. Law provides for city, town, or county liability for property damage if it might have been prevented.

MASSACHUSETTS: No anti-lynching legislation. Property damage to three fourths of the damage done, if more than twelve persons are engaged in the riot.

MICHIGAN: No anti-lynching legislation. Law provides for the transfer of prisoners for safekeeping.

MINNESOTA: Lynching is the killing of a human being, by the act or procurement of a mob. Whenever any person shall be lynched, the county in which said lynching occurred shall be liable in damages to the dependents of the person lynched in a sum not exceeding $7,500, to be recovered in a civil action.

The law further provides that any Sheriff, deputy sheriff, or other officer having custody of any person whom a mob seeks to take from his custody who shall fail or neglect to use all lawful means to resist such taking shall be deemed guilty of malfeasance and shall be removed from office by the Governor.

MISSISSIPPI: No anti-lynching legislation. Prisoners may be removed to another county for safekeeping, or the Sheriff may summon a guard sufficient to protect his prisoner.

MISSOURI: No anti-lynching legislation. Law provides that the Sheriff may employ sufficient guards to protect his prisoner or may move that prisoner to a jail in another county for safekeeping. Liability limited to property damages.

MONTANA: No anti-lynching legislation. Prisoners may be removed to jails in contiguous counties, and cities and towns are liable for property damage done or caused by mobs or riots within their corporate limits.

NEBRASKA: A collection of people assembled for an unlawful purpose and intending to do damage or injury to anyone, or pretending to exercise correctional power over another person by violence and without authority of the law, shall be deemed a "mob" for the purpose of this act. An act of violence resulting in the death of the victim by a mob upon the body of any person shall constitute a "lynching" within the meaning of this act.

The law makes no provisions for the punishment

of lynchers or for the removal of officers for malfeasance. The legal representative of the victim may
sue the county in which the lynching occurred for
damages.

NEVADA: No anti-lynching legislation. Law provides for the removal of prisoners upon written ap-
plication by the Sheriff to the Governor.

NEW HAMPSHIRE: No anti-lynching legislation.
Law provides for removal of prisoners "for such im-
perative and extraordinary purpose." Town's liability
for property loss limited to damage done.

NEW JERSEY: Any collection of individuals, five or
more in number, assembled for the unlawful purpose
of offering violence to the person or property of anyone supposed to have been guilty of a violation of the
law, or for the purpose of exercising correctional
powers or regulative powers over any person or persons by violence, and without lawful authority, shall
be regarded and designated as a "mob."

The penalty for any person or persons who shall
compose a mob as above defined shall be a fine of not
less than $100 or more than $1,000, and he or they
may be imprisoned in the county for a period of not
less than thirty days or to exceed twelve months for
each and every offense. If material damage to the
property or serious injury to the person ensues, the
offender shall be deemed guilty of a felony and shall

suffer imprisonment in the penitentiary for not exceeding five years; and any person so suffering material damage to property or injury to person by a mob shall have an action against the city or county in which such injury is inflicted, for such damages as he may sustain, to an amount not exceeding $5,000. The surviving spouse, lineal heirs, or adopted children may recover from such county or city damages for injury sustained by reason of the loss of life of such person, to a sum not exceeding $5,000.

The law provides for the transfer of prisoners and the removal of the Sheriff for losing his prisoner to a mob.

NEW MEXICO: Anti-lynching legislation confined to assaults on jails. Prisoners may be transferred for safekeeping. The penalty for assault upon jails is, in the case of the death of any jailer, guard, or prisoner, that the offenders upon conviction shall be punished with death. If any jailer, guard, or prisoner be wounded or hurt, the offender, upon conviction, shall be fined in a sum not exceeding $500 or less than $50, or imprisoned for not more than three years nor less than six months, at the discretion of the court.

Provisions are made for the Sheriff's summoning the aid of the people in defending his prisoner and his jail. Failure to aid the Sheriff is punishable by fine or imprisonment or both.

New York: No anti-lynching legislation. City or county's liability for property destroyed by mob violence limited to damage done.

North Carolina: Lynching not clearly defined. Lynching in North Carolina is construed as the illegal entering of a jail for the purpose of killing or injuring a prisoner placed by the law in the Sheriff's custody. The law makes provision for the punishment of witnesses of lynchings who refuse to testify but not for the punishment of the lyncher. Under certain conditions the heirs of the lynch-victim may sue for damages the county wherein the lynching was committed.

North Dakota: No anti-lynching legislation.

Ohio: A collection of people assembled for an unlawful purpose and intending to do damage or injury to anyone, or pretending to exercise correctional power over other persons by violence and without authority of the law, shall be deemed a "mob" for the purpose of this chapter. An act of violence by a mob upon the body of any person shall constitute a "lynching" within the meaning of this chapter.

The act further provides that any person concerned in such lynching may be prosecuted for homicide or assault, and anyone who breaks or attempts to break into a jail or prison, or attacks or attempts to attack an officer with intent to seize a prisoner for the purpose of lynching him, shall be imprisoned in the penitentiary for not less than one year or more than ten years.

The legal representative of the victim of the lynching may recover from the county in which the lynching occurred a sum not to exceed $5,000.

OKLAHOMA: No anti-lynching legislation. In case of an emergency, a Sheriff, with the approval of the county commissioners, may appoint additional jail guards to protect his prisoner.

OREGON: No anti-lynching legislation.

PENNSYLVANIA: "The putting to death, within any county, of any person within the jurisdiction of the county by mob or riotous assemblage of three persons or more, openly acting in concert in violation of the law, and in default of protection of such person by such county or the officers thereof, shall be deemed a denial to such person by such county of the equal protection of the laws, and a violation of the peace of the Commonwealth and an offense against the same.

"Every person participating in such mob or riotous assemblage by which said person is put to death, as described in the section immediately preceding, shall be guilty of murder.

"Every county in which such unlawful putting to death occurs shall be subject to a forfeiture of ten thousand dollars, which may be recovered, by action therefor in the name of the Commonwealth, against such county for the use of the dependent family, if any, of the person so put to death, and, if none, for the use of the Commonwealth. . . ."

The act further debars mob members, pro-lynching advocates, or anyone who has ever entertained or expressed any opinions in favor of lynching, from serving as jurors. Officers who suffer their prisoners to be taken from them by lynch mobs shall be deemed guilty of felony, and, upon conviction, shall be punished by imprisonment for not exceeding five years, or by a fine not exceeding $5,000, or both.

RHODE ISLAND: No anti-lynching legislation. Law provides for transfer of prisoners.

SOUTH CAROLINA: The South Carolina code provides no punishment for lynchers. If a Sheriff, through negligence, permission, or connivance, permits his prisoner to be taken from him for purpose of lynching, he is to be deemed guilty of a misdemeanor, and, upon a true bill being found, shall be deposed from office, and, upon conviction, unless pardoned by the Governor, be ineligible to hold any office of trust or profit within this state.

In all cases of lynching when death ensues, the county where such lynching takes place shall, without regard to the conduct of the officers, be liable in exemplary damages of not less than $2,000, to be recovered by action instituted in any court of competent jurisdiction by the legal representatives of the person lynched.

SOUTH DAKOTA: No anti-lynching legislation.

TENNESSEE: No anti-lynching legislation. A Sheriff who loses his prisoner to a lynch mob through negligence, or by want of proper diligence, firmness, and promptness shall be guilty of a high misdemeanor in office, and, upon conviction thereof, shall be fined at the discretion of the court, forfeit his office, and be declared forever incapable of holding any office of trust or profit in the state.

TEXAS: No anti-lynching legislation. The law provides for the transfer of prisoners to another jail for safekeeping and the employment of additional guards to protect prisoners and jails. Change of venue is provided for in cases of rape.

UTAH: No anti-lynching legislation. The Sheriff may, with the written assent of the district judge, employ additional temporary guards.

VERMONT: No anti-lynching legislation. Law provides for transfer of prisoners for safekeeping.

VIRGINIA: A collection of people, assembled for the purpose and with the intention of committing an assault and/or battery upon any person without authority of the law, shall be deemed a "mob" for the purpose of this act; and any act of violence by a "mob" upon the body of any person, which shall result in the death of such person, shall constitute a "lynching" within the meaning of this act.

The lynching of any person within this state by a "mob" shall be deemed murder, and any and every person composing a "mob" and any and every accessory thereto, by which any person is lynched, shall be guilty of murder, and, upon conviction, shall be punished as provided in chapter 178 of the Code of Virginia.[3] It shall be the duty of the attorney, for the Commonwealth, of any county or city in which a "lynching" may occur, to promptly and diligently endeavor to ascertain the identity of the persons who in any way participated therein, or who composed the "mob" that perpetrated the same, and have them apprehended, and to promptly proceed with the prosecution of any and all persons so found; and to the end that such offenders may not escape proper punishment, such attorney for the Commonwealth may be assisted in all such endeavors and prosecutions, by the Attorney General, or other prosecutors designated by the Governor for the purpose; and the Governor shall have full authority to spend such sums as he may deem necessary for the purpose of

[3] Death.

seeking out the identity and apprehending the members of such guilty "mob."

Nothing herein contained shall be construed to relieve any member of any such mob from civil liability to the personal representative of the victim of such lynching.

The law makes no provision for the punishment of peace officers who release their prisoners to lynch mobs.

WASHINGTON: No anti-lynching legislation.

WEST VIRGINIA: (1) Any collection of individuals, five or more in number, assembled for the unlawful purpose of offering violence to the person or property of anyone supposed to have been guilty of a violation of the law, or for the purpose of exercising correctional powers or regulative powers over any person or persons by violence, and without lawful authority, shall be regarded and designated as a "mob" or "riotous assemblage." (3) The putting to death of any person within this state by a mob or riotous assemblage shall be murder, and every person participating in such mob or riotous assemblage by which a person is put to death shall be guilty of murder, and, upon conviction thereof, shall be punished as provided by chapter 144 of Hogg's Code of West Virginia.[4]

[4] Death.

(6) The county in which such person charged with a crime and within which such person has been taken from a state, county, or municipal officer and lynched and put to death shall be subject to forfeiture of $5,000, which may be recovered by appropriate action therefor, in the name of the personal representative of the person put to death, for the use of his dependent family or the state. Such action may be brought in any state court.

The law makes no provision for the punishment of peace officers who release their prisoners to lynch mobs.

WISCONSIN: No anti-lynching legislation. The county shall be liable for injury to person or property by a mob or riot therein, except that within cities the city shall be liable. This section shall not apply to property damages to houses of ill-fame when the owner has notice that they are used as such.

WYOMING: No anti-lynching legislation.

Appendix

LYNCH-EXECUTIONS IN THE UNITED STATES

1882–1937

Year	Total	Blacks	Whites
1882	114		
1883	134		
1884	211		
1885	184		
1886	138		
1887	122		
1888	142		
1889	176		
1890	128		
1891	195		
1892	235		
1893	200		
1894	197		
1895	180		
1896	131		
1897	165		
1898	127		
1899	107		
1900	115		

273

APPENDIX

1901	135		
1902	97		
1903 [1]	104		
	3337	2060	1277
1904	86	79	7
1905	65	60	5
1906	68	64	4
1907	62	59	3
1908	100	92	8
1909	89	75	14
1910	90	80	10
1911	80	72	8
1912	89	86	3
1913	86	85	1
1914	74	69	5
1915	145	99	46
1916	72	65	7
1917	54	52	2
1918	67	63	4
1919	83	79	4
1920	65	57	8
1921	64	58	6
1922	61	54	7
1923	28	26	2
1924	16	16	0
1925	18	18	0
1926	34	29	5

[1] Estimates to 1903 from Cutler: *Lynch-Law*. After 1904 from the National Association for the Advancement of Colored People.

1927	18	16	2
1928	11	10	1
1929	12	8	4
1930	25	24	1
1931	14	13	1
1932	10	8	2
1933	28	24	4
1934	16	16	0
1935	25	23	2
1936	12	10	2
1937	8	8	0
	5112	3657	1455

Bibliography

Books and Pamphlets

ADAMIC, LOUIS. *Dynamite: the Story of Class Violence in America.* Revised Edition. New York: 1934.

An American Lynching. Being the Burning at the Stake of Henry Lowry at Nodena, Arkansas, January 26, 1921, as Told in American Newspapers. The National Association for the Advancement of Colored People. New York: n.d.

BANCROFT, HUBERT HOWE. "Popular Tribunals," *The Works of Hubert Howe Bancroft,* XXXVI and XXXVII. San Francisco: 1887.

BISHOP, CHARLES M. "The Causes, Consequences and Cure of Mob Violence," *Democracy in Earnest.* Washington: 1918.

BRAWLEY, BENJAMIN. *A Social History of the American Negro.* New York: 1921.

CHADBOURN, JAMES HARMON. *Lynching and the Law.* Chapel Hill: 1933.

CHAPLIN, RALPH. *The Centralia Conspiracy. The Truth About the Armistice Day Tragedy.* General Defense Committee, Chicago: 1924.

COATES, ROBERT M. *The Outlaw Years. The History of the Land Pirates of the Natchez Trace.* New York: 1930.

COLLINS, WINFIELD H. *The Truth About Lynching and the Negro in the South.* New York: 1918.

CUTLER, JAMES ELBERT. *Lynch-Law: an Investigation into the History of Lynching in the United States.* New York: 1905.*

Reprinted 1969 by Patterson Smith, Montclair, New Jersey

DELANEY, ED., AND RICE, M. T. *The Bloodstained Trail.* The Industrial Workers of the World. n.p. n.d.

HAYWOOD, HARRY, AND HOWARD, MILTON. *Lynching: a Weapon of National Oppression.* Labor Research Association Pamphlet #25. New York: 1932.

HEADLEY, J. T. *Pen and Pencil Sketches of the Great Riots.* New York: n.d. (c. 1881).

Lynching of Claude Neal, The. Report of the National Association for the Advancement of Colored People. New York: n.d.

McMASTER, JOHN BACH. *A History of the People of the United States from the Revolution to the Civil War.* 8 v. New York: 1883–1913.

———— *A History of the People of the United States During Lincoln's Administration.* New York: 1927.

NATIONAL ASSOCIATION FOR THE ADVANCEMENT OF COLORED PEOPLE. *Thirty Years of Lynching in the United States, 1889–1918.*

———— Annual Reports, 1919–1936.

RAPER, ARTHUR F. *The Tragedy of Lynching.* Chapel Hill: 1933.*

SHINN, C. H. *Mining Camps: a Study of American Frontier Government.* New York: 1885.

SPIVAK, JOHN L. *Georgia Nigger.* New York: 1932.*

THOMAS, JULIAN B. "A True Story of How the Avenging of the Murder of Chief of Police David C. Hennessey of New Orleans Wiped Out the Mafia in the Crescent City." Unpublished Manuscript.

VICTOR, ORVILLE J. *History of American Conspiracies: a Record of Treason, Insurrection, Rebellion, etc. in the United States of America, from 1760 to 1860.* New York: n.d. (c. 1863).

Reprinted 1969 by Patterson Smith, Montclair, New Jersey

WHITE, WALTER. *Rope and Faggot. A Biography of Judge Lynch.* New York: 1929.

WORK, MONROE N., Editor. *The Negro Year Book, 1937–1938.* Tuskegee: 1937.

Magazine References

Frank Case, the Leo: "Mob Law In Georgia," *Literary Digest*, August 28, 1915; "The Case of Leo M. Frank," *Outlook*, May 26, 1915; "An Outlaw State," *Outlook*, August 25, 1915; "Georgia's Shame," *Independent*, August 30, 1915; "A Georgian Investigation," *Harpers Weekly*, October 2, 1915.

NEA, F. M. "Southern Lynchings," *Nation*, LVI, 407.

"A Double Lynching in Virginia," *Independent*, LII, 783.

POE, C. H. "Lynching: A Southern View," *Atlantic*, XCIII, 155.

"Anarchy in Delaware,": *Outlook*, LXXIV, 543.

"Somerville: Some Cooperating Causes of Negro Lynching." *North American Review*, CLXXVII, 506.

TABER, S. R. "A Remedy for Lynching," *Nation*, LXXV, 478.

"The Rev. Q. Ewing on Lynching," *Independent*, VIII, 2059.

McSWAIN. "What Shall Be Done With Mobs?" *Central Law Journal*, LXVII, 375.

"The Cause of Lynching," *Nation*, LXL, 463.

WELL-BARNETT. "Lynch Law in America," *Arena*, XXIII, 15.

GOEBEL, JULIUS. "The International Responsibility of States for Injuries Sustained by Aliens on Account of Mob Violence, Insurrections and Civil War," *American Journal of International Law*, VIII, 851.

"A Mexican Boycott," *Independent*, LXIX, 1111.

"Lynching: An American Kultur," *New Republic*, XIV, 311.

"Lynching, a National Evil," *Outlook*, CXXXII, 596.

NASH, ROY. "Lynching of Anthony Crawford," *Independent*, LXXXVIII, 456.

DYER. "The Constitutionality of a Federal Anti-Lynching Law," *St. Louis Law Review*, XIII, 186.

"Lynching and Federal Law," *Chautauquan*, XL, 408.

"New Phases of the Fight Against Lynching," *Current Opinion*, LXVII, 45.

MATTHEWS, ALBERT. "The Term Lynch Law," *Modern Philology*, II, 2.

TYREE. "The Origin of Lynching," *Green Bag*, XXV, 393.

"An Inquiry Regarding Lynchings," *South Atlantic Quarterly*, I, 4.

"Lynchings and International Peace," *Outlook*, C, 554.

RANDOLPH, THOMAS. "The Governor and the Mob," *Independent*, LXXXIX, 347.

"The Leavenworth Lynching," *Review of Reviews*, XXIII, 262.

YOUNG, EARL F. "The Relation of Lynching to the Size of Political Areas," *Sociology and Social Research*, XII, 348.

"Rewards to Catch Lynchers," *Nation*, CVII, 218.

"Lynchings and Southern Sentiment," *Outlook*, LXII, 200.

POLL. "The Prevention of Lynch-Law Epidemics," *Review of Reviews*, XVII, 321.

"The Kentucky Cure for Lynching," *Literary Digest*, LXIV, 20.

"How Tampa Treats Lynchers," *Literary Digest*, XCIII, 12.

"The Urbana Lynching," *Public Opinion*, XXII, 741.

"The March of Anarchy," *The New England Magazine*, VII (November, 1834), 409.

"Lynching and Mobs," *American Journal of Social Sciences*, XXXII (November, 1894), 67.

"Negro Outrage no Excuse for Lynching," *Forum*, XVI (November, 1893), 300.

PAGE, WALTER H. "The Last Hold of the Southern Bully," *Forum*, XVI (November, 1893), 303.

"The Epidemic of Savagery," *Outlook*, September 7, 1901.

PAGE, THOMAS NELSON. "The Lynching of Negroes," *North American Review*, January, 1904.

PELL, E. LEIGH. "Prevention of Lynch Law Epidemics," *Review of Reviews*, March, 1898.

LEVELL, WILLIAM HAYNE. "On Lynching in the South." *Outlook*, November 16, 1901.

"Lynching," *Outlook*, XCIII, 637.

"Lynchers Triumphant," *Nation*, XCIII, 386.

BAKER, RAY STANNARD. "What is Lynching? A Study of Mob Justice," *McClure's*, XXIV, 300.

"The Shame of Pennsylvania," *Independent*, LXXI, 437.

"The Practice of Lynching," *Century*, CXV, 65.

"Lynching," *American Law Review*, XLIV, 202.

CLARK, WALTER. "The True Remedy for Lynch Law," *American Law Review*, XXVIII, 802.

Files

The Liberator, edited by William Lloyd Garrison. Boston: 1831–1865.

Niles Weekly Register, edited by H. Niles. Baltimore: 1811–1849.

The Crisis. Volumes 1 to 44; New York: 1910–1937.

The New York Times.

The New York Herald-Tribune.

Index

of Negroes, 133, of women, 133, multiple, 133, since Armistice, 134, at Shelbyville, 134; Anti-lynching legislation, 261-262

Kirby, Will, lynched, 249

Knoxville, Tennessee, lynchings at, 130-131

Ku Klux Klan, 17, 72-75, 87, 136-137, 222, 226, 235-245

Kuykendall, Judge, 106

Lake City, Florida, lynchings at, 128-130

Lakeland, Florida, lynching at, 243-245

Lampson, E. P., lynched, 141

Lawless, Judge, 54-56

Lee, Newt, 153, 154

Lexington, Miss., lynching at, 48, 49

Liberator, The, 33, 44-45, 53, 62, 63

Lincoln, Abraham, 58, 59

Lindsay, Louisiana, lynching at, 119-120

Little, Frank, lynched, 141, 223

Little River, Arkansas, lynching at, 126

Little Rock, Arkansas, lynching at, 126

Lonely Gulch, Arizona, lynching at, 69

Long, Boisey, 128-129

Long, Stella, lynched, 129

Louisiana: Lynchings: early, 60, recorded total, 119, of Negroes, 119, between 1871-73, 74, of women, 119, 121, multiple, 119, at Caddo Parish, 82-83, of John Hastings, his son and daughter, 119, of a lunatic, 119-120, at Sylvester Station, 120-121, of William Gordon, 121, of Laura Porter, 121, Mafia case, 161-168; Anti-lynching legislation, 262

Lovejoy, Reverend Elijah F., 56-59

Lowman, Bertha, lynched, 136-137

Lowman, Demon, lynched, 136-137

Lowman, Sam, 136

Lowry, Henry, lynched, 93, 168-178

Lynch, Colonel Charles, 15, 20-26

Lynch, G. W., lynched, 132

Lynch's Law, 20, 24-25

Lynching defined, 7-10, 254-272

MacDaniels, "Boat Jack," lynched, 247

Mafia, in New Orleans, 161-168

Maine: One lynching, 150; Anti-lynching legislation, 262

Malfeasance of Law Officers, 87-88, 93, 94, 117, 118, 136-137, 149, 153-161, 170-178, 182-184, 191-197, 211-214, 239, 248, 249-250

Marianna, Florida, lynching of Claude Neal, 93, 178-187

Marietta, Georgia, lynching of Leo Frank, 153-161

Marion, Indiana, lynching at, 143-144

Marshall, Richard, lynched, 113

Marshall, Robert, lynched, 150

Maryland: Total recorded lynchings, 146: of Negroes, 146, between 1871-73, 75, of Matt Williams, 94, 146, of George Armwood, 146-147, 207; Anti-lynching legislation, 262

Maryville, Missouri, lynching at, 92, 94

Massachusetts: No lynchings, 100; Anti-lynching legislation, 262

McBride, Sebastian, lynched, 110

McIllherron, Jim, lynched, 132-133

McIntosh, lynched, 54-56

McRae, Governor of Arkansas, 170-178

Memphis, Tennessee, lynchings at, 93, 130, 131

Rolph, Governor James of California, 215-216, 219
Rome, Tennessee, lynching at, 131
Roosevelt, Franklin D., 220
Rosario, Maria del, lynched, 64-65

St. Charles, Arkansas, lynchings at, 126
St. Joseph, Missouri, lynching at, 216-219
St. Louis, Mo., lynching at, 54-56
Salisbury, Maryland, lynching of Matt Williams, 94, 146
Salt City, Georgia, lynching at, 107
San Benito, Texas, lynchings at, 115
San Diego, California, lynching at, 64
San Jose, California, lynching at, 144
Scott, Marie, lynched, 138
Scottsboro Case, 125
Shelbyville, Kentucky, lynchings at, 134
Shelbyville, Tennessee, mob repulsed, burns courthouse down, 133
Sherman, Texas, lynching at, 117-118, 197-206
Shoemaker, Joseph, 223-243
Sholtz, Governor Dave, of Florida, 240
Shreveport, Louisiana, lynchings at, 119
Shuman, Simon, lynched, 111
Slaton, Governor of Georgia, 157, 158
Smith, Henry, lynched, 92
South Carolina: Lynchings: recorded total, 135, between 1871-73, 74, of Negroes, 135, of women, 135, multiple, 135, since Armistice, 135; Anti-lynching legislation, 268-269
South Dakota: See North and South Dakota

South Point, Ohio, lynching at, 147
South Sulphur, Texas, lynching at, 60
Southampton massacre, 33, 37-45
Southern Commission on the Study of Lynching, 10
Squire Birch, 18, 19, 51, 52
Statesboro, Georgia, lynchings at, 110, 111
Sylvester Station, Louisiana, lynching at, 120-121

Tallahassee, Florida, lynchings at, 248
Talullah, Louisiana, lynchings at, 119
Tampa, Florida, lynchings at, 128, 234-245
Tennessee: Lynchings: early, 61, recorded total, 130, between 1871-73, 74, of Negroes, 130, of women, 130, multiple, 130, since Armistice, 130, at Clarksdale, 83, of Ell Person, 93, 130-131, at Tiptonville, Memphis, Chattanooga, Nashville, Knoxville, Ripley, Rome, 130-131, of Ben Pettigrew, 131, of Jim McIllherron, 132-133, of Albert Gooden, 248-249; Anti-lynching legislation, 269
Texas: Lynchings: early, 53, recorded total, 114, of Negroes, 114, of women, 114, multiple, 114, at South Sulphur, 60, at San Benito, 69, at Paris, 92, of Reverend Captain Jones, 114, of Dan Davis, 116, of Jesse Washington, 116-117, of two Negro minors, 117, of George Hughes, 98, 118, 197-206; Anti-lynching legislation, 269
Thomas, T. J., lynched, 113
Thompson, Gilbert, lynched, 111
Thompson, Will, lynched, 111

INDEX

Thurmond, Thomas H., lynched, 144, 212-216
Tiptonville, Tennessee, lynchings at, 130
Torture, 94-98, 103, 104, 108-109, 110, 111-112, 116, 117, 118, 120-121, 131-133, 142, 149, 175-178, 184-185, 196-197, 201-203, 225, 231-233, 238, 239, 247
Townes, Roosevelt, lynched, 247
Turner, Hayes, lynched, 111
Turner, Mary, lynched, 107, 111-112
Turner, Nat, 37-43
Tuskegee, Department of Records and Research, 10
Tyler, Texas, lynching at, 116
Tyronne, R. J., lynched, 105

United Citrus Workers' Union, 243
Utah: Lynchings: recorded total, 150, of Negroes, 150, of Robert Marshall, 150, of Joe Hill, 223; Anti-lynching legislation, 269

Vaughan, Sheriff, delivered Albert Gooden to mob, 248-249
Vehmgerichte of Westphalia, 16, 17
Vermont: No lynchings, 100; Anti-lynching legislation, 269
Vesey, Denmark, 35-37
Vicksburg, Miss., lynchings at, 49-51, 101
Vigilantes, 17, 65-69, 141-142
Virginia: Lynchings: recorded total, 139, between 1871-73, 74, of Negroes, 139, of women, 139, multiple, 139, since Armistice, 140; Anti-lynching legislation, 269-270

Waco, Texas, lynching at, 116-117
Walker, David, 31, 32

Walker, Zachariah, lynched, 149
Warner, Lloyd, lynched, 216-219
Washington: Lynchings: recorded total, 146, of Negroes, 146, since Armistice, 146, of Wesley Everest, 146, 226-233; Anti-lynching legislation, 271
Washington, Jesse, lynched, 116-117
Watson, Thomas E., 154, 158-159
Watts, Foster, lynched, 112
West, Jack, lynched, 78
West Virginia: Lynchings: recorded total, 142-143, of Negroes, 142, of women, 142, since Armistice, 143, of Mrs. T. Arthur, 142, of Robert Johnson, 143; Anti-lynching legislation, 271-272
White, Governor Hugh of Mississippi, 245, 247-248
White, Walter, 10, 127
Williams, Matt, lynched, 94, 146
Wilmington, Delaware, lynching near, 151
Wilson, T. W., District Attorney addresses mob, 93
Wisconsin: Lynchings: recorded total, 150, between 1871-73, 75; Anti-lynching legislation, 272
Women, lynching of, 65, 98, 102-103, 104, 107, 111-112, 114, 119, 124, 126, 127, 129, 130, 131, 133, 135, 136-137, 138, 139, 140, 142
Woodson, Edward, lynched, 144
Work, Monroe N., 10
Workers' Defense League, 10
Wyoming: Lynchings: recorded total, 144, of Negroes, 144, since Armistice, 144, of Edward Woodson, 144; Anti-lynching legislation, 272

Yazoo City, Miss., lynchings at, 101
Young, Ab, lynched, 93

288

PATTERSON SMITH REPRINT SERIES IN
CRIMINOLOGY, LAW ENFORCEMENT, AND SOCIAL PROBLEMS